RUM & REGGAE'S
PUERTO RICO
with Culebra & Vieques

Rum&Reggae's
Puerto Rico
Culebra & Vieques

by

Jonathan Runge

RUM & REGGAE GUIDEBOOKS, Inc. •
Prides Crossing, Massachusetts • 2002

ISBN: 1-893675-07-6
LIBRARY OF CONGRESS CATALOG CARD NUMBER: 2001119641

Book design by Scott-Martin Kosofsky and Betsy Sarles at The Philidor Company, Cambridge, MA

Cover design by Betsy Sarles & Jonathan Runge

Maps by Tony Lulek and Bruce Withey
Printed in Canada on recycled paper

For Bethie

CONTENTS

PUERTO RICO

0　　　　10　　　　20
MILES

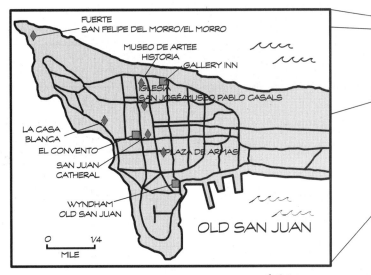

FUERTE
SAN FELIPE DEL MORRO/EL MORRO

MUSEO DE ARTEE
HISTORIA
GALLERY INN

IGLESIA
SAN JOSÉ/MUSEO PABLO CASALS

LA CASA
BLANCA
EL CONVENTO

SAN JUAN
CATHERAL

PLAZA DE ARMAS

WYNDHAM
OLD SAN JUAN

OLD SAN JUAN

0　　　　1/4
MILE

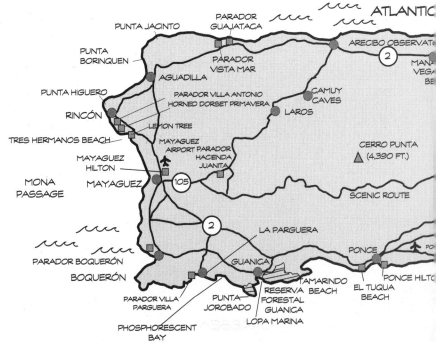

ATLANTIC

PARADOR
GUAJATACA

PUNTA JACINTO

PUNTA
BORINQUEN

PARADOR
VISTA MAR

ARECIBO OBSERVAT

MAN
VEGA
BE

AGUADILLA

PARADOR VILLA ANTONIO
HORNED DORSET PRIMAVERA

CAMUY
CAVES

PUNTA HIGUERO

RINCÓN

LAROS

LEMON TREE

TRES HERMANOS BEACH

CERRO PUNTA
△ (4,390 FT.)

MAYAGUEZ
AIRPORT PARADOR
HACIENDA
JUANITA

MAYAGUEZ
HILTON

MONA
PASSAGE

MAYAGUEZ

105

SCENIC ROUTE

2

LA PARGUERA

PARADOR BOQUERÓN

BOQUERÓN

GUANICA

PONCE

PONCE HILTO

PO

PARADOR VILLA
PARGUERA

PUNTA
JOROBADO

TAMARINDO
BEACH

RESERVA
FORESTAL
GUANICA

EL TUQUA
BEACH

LOPA MARINA

PHOSPHORESCENT
BAY

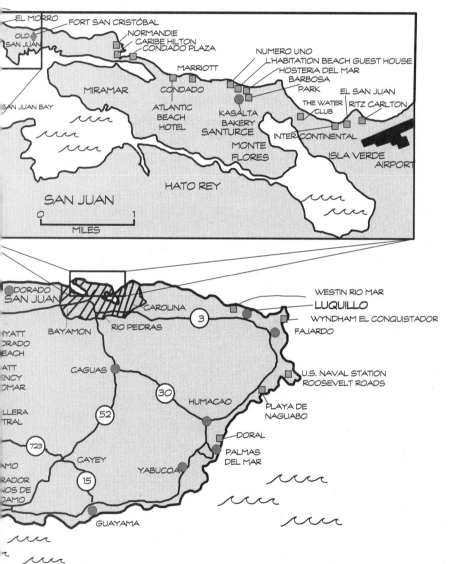

N

SAN JUAN

EL MORRO
OLD SAN JUAN
FORT SAN CRISTÓBAL
NORMANDIE
CARIBE HILTON
CONDADO PLAZA
NUMERO UNO
L'HABITATION BEACH GUEST HOUSE
HOSTERIA DEL MAR
BARBOSA PARK
EL SAN JUAN
RITZ CARLTON
MARRIOTT
MIRAMAR
CONDADO
SAN JUAN BAY
ATLANTIC BEACH HOTEL
KASALTA BAKERY
THE WATER CLUB
SANTURCE
INTER-CONTINENTAL
MONTE FLORES
ISLA VERDE
AIRPORT
HATO REY

0   1
MILES

DORADO
SAN JUAN
CAROLINA
LUQUILLO
WESTIN RIO MAR
WYNDHAM EL CONQUISTADOR
BAYAMON
RIO PEIDRAS
FAJARDO
HYATT DORADO BEACH
HATT ENCY OMAR
CAGUAS
U.S. NAVAL STATION
ROOSEVELT ROADS
LLERA TRAL
HUMACAO
PLAYA DE NAGUABO
723
DORAL
PALMAS DEL MAR
AMO
CAYEY
YABUCOA
RADOR NOS DE DAMO
GUAYAMA

CARIBBEAN SEA

PREFACE

R UM & REGGAE'S PUERTO RICO is the fourth book to be published by Rum & Reggae Guidebooks, Inc. Many readers of the original *Rum & Reggae's Caribbean* will notice that there are now other writers working for the cause. Quite simply, I just couldn't do all the writing and updating by myself anymore. I also have to run the company. Besides, I'm older now and can only schlep for so long. However, rest assured that the information and commentary are as good if not better than previous editions of Rum and Reggae, as I am the editor (and a demanding one at that)!

Besides myself, here's a look at the writers for *Rum & Reggae's Puerto Rico:*

☞ David Swanson is a San Diego–based freelance writer who has been traveling to the Caribbean for the past 16 years. Although he enjoys all of the islands to varying degrees, he has particularly enjoyed discovering the region's more exotic corners, including Haiti, Cuba (in 1989, just as the Soviet Union was dropping aid), and the summit of Montserrat's smoldering volcano. Swanson's work has appeared in more than 45 North American newspapers and assorted magazines, including *Caribbean Travel and Life*, *American Way*, and *National Geographic Traveler*, *Caribbean*, *The Atlanta Journal–Constitution*, biztravel.com, *Bridal Guide*, *Chicago Magazine*, *Islands*, and numerous other publications.

☞ Mark Browne is an independent writer, copywriter, and marketing consultant with clients in the U.S. and Latin America. He is a native of Boston and has traveled extensively throughout the Caribbean and Mexico. He currently lives in Mexico City and can be reached at markb@mbrowne.com.

We hope you enjoy the book. Please be sure to visit our Web site at www.rumreggae.com.

ACKNOWLEDGMENTS

CONTRARY TO WHAT YOU MIGHT THINK, writing a book on Puerto Rico is not very glamorous. The most glittering part about doing it is answering the "So what do you do?" question at cocktail parties. It's all uphill from there. We did not spend our days on the beach or by the pool sipping a piña colada. Well, okay, sometimes we did. But most of the time we were running around checking out this or that and complaining about the heat. Just when we started to get comfortable in a place, it was time to uproot ourselves and start all over again. Try doing that at least every other day and you'll begin to know what we mean.

Fortunately, some wonderful people helped us out along the way. We'd like to take this opportunity to sincerely thank those who did. In no particular order, they are Linda and Burr Vail, Harold Davies and Kingsley Wratten, Wilhelm Sack, Horst Sicher, Ivelis Crespo, Frances Borden, Kim Greiner, and Gay Myers. If we overlooked your name, sorry, but thanks for your help!

Rum & Reggae's Puerto Rico is published by Rum & Reggae Guidebooks, Inc. I have a lot of helpers and all deserve a hearty thanks. First and foremost, a lot of credit for this book goes to David Swanson, my chief Caribbean writer, editor, and general bon vivant of the West Coast. Thanks, too, to my other contributor, Mark Browne. My warmest gratitude also goes to the following: our wonderful book designers, Betsy Sarles and Scott-Martin Kosofsky; our very talented web designer, Michael Carlson; our corporate illustrator and animation megastar, Eric Orner; our cartographers, Bruce Withey and Tony Lulek; our distributor, Midpoint Trade Books and its great staff, Gail Kump, Eric Kampf, Chris Bell, and Julie Borgelt; our printer, Transcontinental Printing, and its terrific rep, Ed Catania; and our patient copy editor and indexer, Judith Antonelli.

There were several people who helped in other ways. Muchas gracias to Nan Garland, Duncan Donahue and Tom Fortier, Elvis Jiménez-Chávez and Chris Lawrence, Tom Jonsson, and Gedy Moody.

Finally, wicked thanks to our staff members, Joe Shapiro—the Director of Marketing and Sales and a Brazil nut; and Lauren White, copy editor, proofreader, and all-around great gal. Tons of thanks also to my business partner and right-hand man, Tony Lulek; and to my parents, Eunice and Albert Runge, for their continued enthusiasm and support.

And a can of dolphin-safe tuna to my cat and guardian angel, Jada.

To all who helped, many thanks—YAH MON!

Jonathan Runge
Author and Publisher
Rum & Reggae Guidebooks, Inc.
Prides Crossing, Massachusetts
March 1, 2002

INTRODUCTION

OUR MIDDLE NAME IS BITCH.™ That's how we describe our distinct point of view. *Rum & Reggae's Puerto Rico* is not your typical tourist guidebook to the Isle of Enchantment. We like to say that the Rum & Reggae series is written for people who want more out of a vacation than the standard tourist fare. Our reader is more sophisticated and independent. He's also more active—be it scuba diving, windsurfing, nightclubbing, hiking, sailing, golfing, playing tennis, exploring, or cocktailing. Or she's more particular, in search of places that are secluded, cerebral, spiritual, or très branché (if you have to ask what the latter means, those places are not for you).

This book differs from other guidebooks in another way. Instead of telling you that everything is "nice"—nice, that is, for the average Joe—*Rum & Reggae's Puerto Rico* offers definitive opinions. We will tell you what's fantastic and what's not, from the point of view of someone who loathes the tourist label and the other bland travel books whose names we won't mention.

We'll take you all over the island and to the Puerto Rican islands of Culebra and Vieques, too. We share our recommendations of where to go (and where not to go). More important, we filter out all the crap for you so you can have fun reading the book and enjoy your vacation and keep the decision making to a minimum. We wish we had this book when we were doing our research. It would have made our job a helluva lot easier. We would have had more time to kick back and get sand between our toes.

So mix yourself a piña colada (don't forget to use fresh pineapple juice), put on some salsa, and sit back and let *Rum & Reggae's Puerto Rico* take you on your own private voyage to the *las islas bonitas*.

BEFORE YOU GO

Climate

The weather in Puerto Rico, Culebra, and Vieques is about as close to perfect as anywhere on Earth. The temperature rarely dips below 70 degrees or scales to above 90 degrees F (at sea level). It can get cooler at night in the mountains of some of the islands, making it ideal for sleeping. The sun shines almost every day. Rainfall comes in the form of brief, intense cloudbursts, quickly followed by sunshine. It's pretty hard not to get a tan.

The reasons for this ideal climate are the constant temperature of the ocean—about 80 degrees F year-round—and the steady trade winds from Africa. The Caribbean is not susceptible to the harsh weather patterns of the middle latitudes. The only weather peril to a Puerto Rico vacation is an occasional summer tropical depression or hurricane, which can make life very exciting.

There are two basic climate categories in Puerto Rico: lush (very green, hot, somewhat humid, with lots of rainfall) and arid (brown with cactus and very dry). The windward side (the north and east coasts) is the lush, wetter, and greener side. The mountains that traverse the center of the island from east to west, the Cordillera Central, block most of the typical rainfall that comes with the prevailing trade winds. This makes the southern and western coasts semi-arid to arid. A striking example of this contrast is readily seen with the drive on Rt. 52 from San Juan to Ponce. The change from verdant to brown happens in just a few miles once the summit of the road is passed.

Culebra and Vieques are very arid islands, due to the lack of mountains to catch the clouds and rainfall. Vegetation is scrubby with cactus, although there certainly are enough palm trees to keep palm tree lovers happy.

Both lush and arid climes are warm to hot, depending on the season and the extent of the trade winds. Summer, while only about five degrees hotter than winter, feels much warmer due to the increased humidity and decreased wind. The one constant is the sun. It is always strong, and will swiftly fry unprotected pale faces—and bodies—to a glowing shade of lobster red.

Building a Base for Tanning

Since the advent of "fake 'n bake" (tanning machines) and pretanning accelerators, there is absolutely no reason to get burned on your first day out in the tropical sun. With some advance attention, you can stay outside for hours on your first day, and let's face it, what you want to do when you step off the plane is hit the beach.

Just about every town has a tanning center with a cutesy name like Tanfastic or Tanfasia. Most health clubs have one or two tanning "coffins" lying around, beckoning pasty skins to look healthier and more attractive in a matter of minutes. Ultraviolet tanning is safe when used properly, because the UVB light doesn't have the severe burning rays of earlier sun lamps or, of course, the sun.

Many of these tanning centers have tanning-prep packages of 10 sessions: you start with about five minutes of "sunning" and work up to 20 or 30. Spread out over the two weeks prior to your departure, this should give you an excellent head start on a great Caribbean tan.

Pretan accelerators, available from a wide variety of manufacturers, chemically stimulate the manufacture of melanin, the pigment that darkens your skin. (Normally it takes direct exposure to the sun to start its production.) A pretan accelerator doesn't change your color or dye your skin like the QT of yesteryear (whoops, we're dating ourselves!). It prepares the skin with extra melanin so that you tan the first time out rather than burn, and much faster, too.

What to Wear and Take Along

Less is more. That's the motto to remember when packing to go to the Caribbean. Bring only what you can carry for 10 minutes at a good clip, because you'll often be schlepping your luggage for at least that time, and it's hot. If you haven't already done so, invest in a piece of luggage with wheels.

What you really need to take along are a bathing suit, shorts, T-shirts or tanks, cotton sweater, a pair of sandals, sunglasses, and a Discman. After all, you are on vacation. However, this is the dawn of a new century and people tend to dress up for no reason, so you may want to bring some extra togs to look presentable at the dinner table. To help you be totally prepared (and to make your packing a lot easier), we've assembled a list of essentials for a week.

The Packing List

Clothes

bathing suit (or two)

T shirts (4)—You'll end up buying at least one.

tank tops—They're cooler and show off your muscles or curves.

polo shirts (2)

shorts (2)

nice, compatible lightweight pants (also good for the plane)

sandals—Those that can get wet, like Tevas, are best.

cotton sweater or sweatshirt

undergarments

sneakers (or good walking shoes) or topsiders (for boaters)

Women: lightweight dress (most women prefer to bring a couple of dresses for evening)

Men: If you must have a lightweight sport coat wear it (with appropriate shoes) on the plane.

Essentials

toiletries

sunscreens (SPF 15+, 8, 4 [oil], and lip protector)

moisturizers (Noxema is still the old standard for sunburn; or aloe gel)

some good books—Don't expect to find a worthwhile read at your destination.

Cutter's or Woodsman's insect repellent, or Skin So Soft (oh, those nasty bugs)

sunglasses!

hat or visor!

Discman (CDs) or iPod

camcorder or pocket camera (disposables are great for the beach and underwater disposables for snorkeling)

"credit card" calculator (for exchange rates)
Sports Accessories (where applicable)
tennis racquet
golf clubs
hiking shoes
fins, mask, snorkel, regulator, and C-card
ATM card and credit cards
driver's license

Puerto Rico Superlatives (includes Culebra & Vieques)

Best Beach—**Playa Flamenco,** Culebra
Best Large Luxury Resort (over 100 rooms)—**Hyatt Dorado Beach**
Best Small Luxury Resort (under 100 rooms)—**Horned Dorset Primivera**
Best Resort for Kids—**Hyatt Cerromar Beach**
Best Romantic Hotel—**Casa Flamboyant,** Naguabo
Best Boutique Hotel— **The Water Club,** Isla Verde
Best Large Hotel—**San Juan Marriot,** Condado
Best Small Hotel—**Numero Uno,** Ocean Park
Best Inn—**Hacienda Tamarindo,** Vieques
Best Eco-Friendly "Green" Hotel—**La Finca Caribe,** Vieques
Best Gay-Friendly Accommodation—**Inn on the Blue Horizon,** Vieques
Best Room with a View—**The Gallery Inn,** Old San Juan
Best Fusion Restaurant—**Pikayo,** Santurce
Best Caribbean-Style Restaurant—**Pamela's,** Ocean Park
Best Latino Nuevo Restaurant—**The Parrot Club,** Old San Juan
Best Puerto Rican Restaurant—**Ajili Mojili,** Old San Juan
Best French Restaurant—**Horned Dorset Primavera,** Rincón
Best Pan-Asian Restaurant—**Dragonfly,** Old San Juan
Best Sushi—**Cherry Blossom,** Condado
Best Italian Restaurant—**Il Perugino,** Old San Juan
Best Steak House—**Ruth's Chris,** Isla Verde
Best Vegetarian Restaurant—**Café Berlin,** Old San Juan
Best Café con Leche—**Kasalta Bakery,** Ocean Park
Best Lunch Spot—**Hosteria del Mar,** Ocean Park

Best Piña Colada—**The Terrace Bar,** Caribe Hilton
Best Place for a Sunset Cocktail—**Horned Dorset Primavera,**
  Rincón
Best Nightclub—**Stargate,** San Juan
Best Gay Nightclub—**Eros,** San Juan
Best Place for Nightlife—**San Juan**
Best Place for Gay Nightlife—**San Juan**
Best Diving—**Culebra**
Best Snorkeling—**Culebrita**
Best Camping—**Playa Flamenco,** Culebra
Best Golf Course—**Hyatt Dorado Beach**
Best Hike—**El Yunque**
Best Tennis—**Hyatt Cerromar**
Best Windsurfing—**Rincón**
Best Shopping—**Old San Juan**
Best T-Shirt—**Mamacita's,** Culebra
Best Bargain—**the guest houses** of Ocean Park
Best-Kept Secret—**Culebra**

The Ten Best Beaches in Puerto Rico, Culebra, and Vieques

Playa Flamenco—Culebra
  An almost perfect crescent of blindingly white sand, often with
  body-surfable waves in the wintertime.
Ocean Park—Santurce, PR
  Probably the best city beach in the Caribbean, the sand is pow-
  dery and the breezes steady.
Boquerón—PR
  A beautiful crescent of golden sand on a tranquil bay, best on
  weekdays.
Navio Beach—Vieques
  Very quiet, we still can't get over how blue the water is here.
Playa Succia—Cabo Rojo, PR
  A well-kept secret just east of the Faro de Cabo Rojo.
Sun Bay—Vieques
  We like this long crescent because it's big, is close to town, and
  has facilities.

Luquillo—PR

One of the prettiest beaches on the north coast, it's still lovely despite encroaching development. Trade winds keep it cool, too.

Guánica Forest Reserve—PR

Lots of small, private beach coves facing an island of picturesque palms.

Crash Boat—Aguadilla, PR

Great place to watch the best surfing in PR.

Playa Soni—Culebra

Always empty, this white-sand beach faces a tranquil bay and Culebrita.

Lodging and Restaurant Key

A Note about this Guide: We have used a number of symbols and terms to indicate prices and ambiance. Here are the code breakers.

Lodging Rates

☞ Rates are for high season—generally mid-December through mid-April—unless otherwise noted. Summer prices are as much as 50 percent cheaper.

☞ The following categories correspond to rack rates for the least expensive double room. Unless otherwise noted. Rates for singles are the same or slightly less.

☞ Expect a service and tax charge of at least 15 percent added to your bill. Some countries can reach 25 percent! Ouch! Be sure to ask ahead of time to avoid going into shock. (Ask at the front desk how the service charge will be distributed to employees—usually you are not expected to leave any additional tips.)

☞ Be sure to ask about credit cards when making your reservations if you intend to use them as payment. A few places, even expensive ones, do not accept credit cards.

Dirt Cheap	under $50
Cheap	$51–$100
Not So Cheap	$101–$150

Pricey	$151–$200
Very Pricey	$201–$300
Wicked Pricey	$301–$400
Ridiculous	$401–$500
Beyond Belief	$501–$600
Stratospheric	$601 and up!

Meal Codes

EP (European Plan)—No meals included.

CP (Continental Plan)—Continental breakfast (bread, cereal, juice, coffee) included.

BP (Breakfast Plan)—Full hot breakfast included.

MAP(Modified American Plan)—Full breakfast and dinner included.

FAP (Full American Plan)—Full breakfast, lunch, and dinner included (sometimes with an afternoon "tea" or snack as well).

All-Inclusive All meals, beer, wine, and well drinks (house brands) are included, most or all on-site activities, and usually tax and service charges.

Restaurant Prices

Prices represent per-person cost for the average meal from soup to nuts.

$	$0–$10
$$	$11–$20
$$$	$21–$30
$$$$	$31–$40
$$$$$	over $40

Touristo Scale Key

(1)

What century is this?

(2)

Tiny or no airport, or political upheaval keeps tourists away.

(3)

A nice, unspoiled yet civilized place.

(4)

Still unspoiled, but getting popular.

(5)

A popular place, but still not too developed.

(6)

Busy and booming; this was very quiet not long ago.

(7)

Well-developed tourism and lots of tourists;
fast-food outlets conspicuous.

(8)

Highly developed and tons of tourists.

(9)

Mega-tourists, and tour groups;
fast-food outlets outnumber restaurants.

(10)

Swarms of tourists and total development. Run for cover!

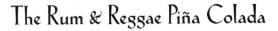

The Rum & Reggae Piña Colada

Ingredients
1 ounce Coco López (or any coconut cream)
1 ounce heavy cream (yes, this is a fattening drink!)
2 ounces of light rum (preferably Bicardi or Don Q)
2 ounces unsweetened pineapple juice (fresh is best)

Directions
Mix with 2/3 cup crushed ice in blender until creamy smooth. Garnish with a slice of fresh pineapple and a cherry (the latter just for the visual). Enjoy!

Rum & Reggae Punch

Are you dreaming of the tropics but it's snowing outside? Don't worry, you can create your own heat with this recipe.

Ingredients
1 lime
4 oz. water
2–3 oz. good dark rum (the stronger, the better)
2 oz. sugar syrup*
bitters
ice
freshly grated nutmeg

Directions
Squeeze the lime and add the juice and water to the rum and sugar syrup in a tall glass. Shake bitters into the glass four times. Add the rocks, then sprinkle with freshly grated nutmeg (it must be fresh!). Yum! Serves one.

----

*To make sugar syrup, combine 1 lb. sugar and 2 cups of water in a saucepan. Boil for about 2 minutes for sugar to dissolve. Let cool. Keep handy for quick and easy rum punches.

PUERTO RICO

Touristo Scale: 👤 👤 👤 👤 👤 👤 👤 👤 👤 (9)

Overview

I t happens every time, without fail. As soon as the jet's wheels touch down at San Juan's Luis Muñoz Marín International Airport, there is a burst of applause. The Puerto Ricans on the plane are very happy. The trip has ended safely and they are home. This ritual always causes us to chuckle, it's so genuine that even our jaded cynicism melts away. And hell, we're also pleased to be here 'cuz we just *love* Puerto Rico. Why? Well, besides the the beautiful and diverse island, because of the people. Puerto Ricans, also called *Boriquas* (the Taíno or Indian name), are very happy, warm people who seem to always be up and wanting to have a good time. Party seems to be their collective middle name. Puerto Rico is a big island, roughly the size of Connecticut. There are 3.8 million people, a major metropolis, a diverse economy, mountains, rain forest, miles of beautiful beaches, the hip swaying beat of salsa, and the she-bang hip thrusts of Ricky Martin. Being a Commonwealth of the United States, the American influence is very pervasive—from every conceivable fast-food and convenience chain (there are more than 50 Burger Kings on the island) to the huge pharmaceutical and high-tech companies. This is unfortunate but inevitable. Yet the culture is still Latino and the language is still Spanish, although most Puerto Ricans speak English or at least understand it to a degree. Former Governor Pedro Roselló reinstated the policy that Puerto Rico officially has two languages—Spanish and English—to encourage bilingualism among the populace and inch the island toward statehood. More often than not, however, you'll hear and marvel at the hybrid, commonly known as "Spanglish."

Most visitors who come to Puerto Rico see only San Juan, a

1

metro area of over 1.6 million people (residents are referred to as *Sanjuaneros*) or just its airport. This is where most of the big hotels and casinos are located. San Juan is also the second-largest cruise-ship port after Miami. The combination ensures lots of tourists, especially in places like Old San Juan and Isla Verde. But San Juan is a big city, and with it comes the best nightlife (both straight and gay) in the Caribbean. If you want great restaurants, big and lively casinos (without the Las Vegas tackiness), pulsating nightclubs, and to mix with some of the hottest men and women you'll ever meet—look no further for your next vacation spot. If you're single, you're crazy not to go here. But you must like Latinos and Latinas (you're even crazier if you don't). And Puerto Ricans are *very* Latin when it comes to romance. If you haven't had a Latin lover, we'll be the first to tell you—they invented the words "heat" and "passion." There's an ad slogan that says "Puerto Rico Does It Better." There should be another one that says "Puerto Ricans Do It Better"!

But there is much more to Puerto Rico than the throbbing beat of San Juan. There are beautiful mountains and lush valleys, and small seaside towns with lots of character, like Boquerón and Guánica. There is Puerto Rico's second city, Ponce, which has undergone a restoration similar to Old San Juan. There are the twin resorts of Dorado Beach and Cerromar Beach with some of the best golf and tennis in the Caribbean. There are the extraordinary Camuy Caves—huge natural caverns several hundred feet in the earth. There is great windsurfing off Rincón on the west coast. There are the unspoiled out-islands of Culebra and Vieques (detailed in their own chapters). There is the Caribbean National Forest, "El Yunque," which is an easily accessed rain forest. There are deserted beaches on all sides of the island. But you're never more than a two-hour drive from San Juan or far from an ATM and a Big Gulp from 7-Eleven.

Puerto Rico gets all kinds of tourists and travelers. There are the convention and tour groups who come for a purpose as well as to play in the big casinos and on the beach. The cruise ships flood Old San Juan with that element of middle America that loves outlet shopping and always seems devoid of fashion sense. (Don't these people read *W* or the *Men's Fashion* supplement of *The New York Times*?) There are lots of European tourists, especially Germans, and rich South Americans up on shopping sprees. Of course, most of the visitors here are American. Then there are the independent travelers who dive into the culture and countryside in search of the real Puerto Rico, and the long-weekenders down for a dose of sun and fun since San Juan is so easy (and cheap) to reach.

The Briefest History

Puerto Rico was first settled by Taíno Amerindians who ventured up the chain of West Indies from the Amazon and South America. They had been on the island for thousands of years when Columbus landed here on his second voyage, in 1493. He discovered about 60,000 Taíno Amerindians, living off the land and sea, who had named the island Boriquen. Spain claimed the island and Columbus called it San Juan, later renamed Puerto Rico. With Columbus was Juan Ponce de León, Mr. Fountain of Youth himself, who sensed gold in "them-thar hills" and received permission to colonize the island. The first Spanish settlement began in 1508 at Caparra, and Ponce de León became its governor. But that site proved disease-ridden, so in 1521 the settlement was moved to what is now Old San Juan. It became a fortress with El Morro fort at its entrance. Spain never lost control of Puerto Rico for more than 400 years, despite repeated attempts by the British, French, and Dutch to dislodge them. It wasn't until the Spanish-American War in 1898, when Teddy Roosevelt led the charge up that hill in Havana shouting "Remember the *Maine*" and defeated the Spanish, that control ceded to another power. That power was the United States. In 1917 Puerto Ricans became full-fledged U.S. citizens, and in 1952 Puerto Rico became a Commonwealth of the United States. It remains so today. There is an ongoing drive for statehood, which is being spearheaded by the current governor. The most recent plebiscite voted to keep the status quo. Under Commonwealth status, Puerto Ricans have a U.S. passport and can live anywhere in the U.S. They have local representation in a Commonwealth government and pay no federal income tax as residents of Puerto Rico (however, they do pay P.R. government income taxes). The drawback to Commonwealth status is that they have no voting representation in Congress (they can't vote for president, either). However, there is a nonvoting Interests Section in Congress. But no federal taxes and no sales tax—what a deal. We're moving to Puerto Rico!

Puerto Rico: Key Facts

LOCATION	18°N by 65°W
	70 miles east of Hispaniola (Dominican Republic)
	1,040 miles southeast of Miami
	1,662 miles southeast of New York
SIZE	3,423 square miles
	110 miles long by 35 miles wide
HIGHEST POINT	Cerro de Punta (4,390 ft.)
POPULATION	3.92 million
LANGUAGES	Spanish (English is officially the second language and is widely spoken in San Jaun)
TIME	Atlantic Standard Time (1 hour ahead of EST, same as EDT)
AREA CODE	787 (must be dialed before all local numbers as well)
ELECTRICITY	110 volts ac, same as U.S. and Canada
CURRENCY	The U.S. dollar
DRIVING	On the *right*
DOCUMENTS	None for Americans and no Customs hassles either; Canadians need proof of nationality or a passport; Brits need a passport and visa
DEPARTURE TAX	None
BEER TO DRINK	Medalla
RUM TO DRINK	Don Q or Bacardi
MUSIC TO HEAR	Salsa!
TOURISM INFO	787-721-2400, www.prtourism.com or http://welcome.topuertorico.org

Getting There

Of all the Caribbean islands, Puerto Rico is the easiest to reach. San Juan has a huge international airport (Luis Muñoz Marín), which is the hub of **American**'s Caribbean operation, has more than thirty airlines serving it, and receives over 400 nonstops weekly from the U.S. Most major eastern and southern cities have nonstop service to San Juan on **American, Continental, Delta, Northwest, United, US Airways,** and **American Trans Air.** From Canada, connections can be made on several U.S. carriers from Montreal and Toronto, there is service on **Canadian Airlines.** From Europe, **British Airways, Ibéria,** and **AirFrance** all have nonstop service. **American Eagle** and **LIAT,** fly to neighboring islands.

Getting Around

With just about every major rental car player here offering great weekly (and daily) rates, and with so much to see, it makes perfect sense to rent a car. **Avis** (800-331-1084 or 787-253-5926), **Budget** (800-527-0700 or 787-791-3685), **Hertz** (800-654-3001 or 787-791-0840), **National** (800-227-3876), and **Thrifty** (800-367-2277) are all here. Call your favorite for reservations. In addition, several local companies may offer you a better rate; try **Charlie Car Rental** (787-728-2418) and **L&M Car Rental** (787-791-1160). Check with your credit card company to see what your coverage includes before you rent.

The Puerto Rican Tourism Company has instituted a welcome and easy-to-use taxi system at the airport and in the major tourist areas. Outside the Baggage Claim, there is a taxi stand with several representatives of the P.R.T.C. (they have the "Puerto Rico Does It Better" buttons on as well as IDs). The cabs are painted white with "Taxi Touristicos" and the official logo painted on the front doors. Fixed rates apply to the major tourist zones. Longer trips are metered. A cab ride from the airport to Isla Verde is $8, to the Condado area is $12, and to Old San Juan is $16 (not including tip).

Within San Juan, there is a good bus system run by the Metropolitan Bus Authority, 787-767-7979. The buses (called *guaguas*) pick up passengers at upright yellow post stops (called *paradas*), and the fare is 25¢ or 50¢.

Públicos (public cars) are cars or minivans that provide low-cost transportation to the main towns in Puerto Rico. Their rates are set by the Public Service Commission. For information call 787-756-1919.

Some words about driving in Puerto Rico: Puerto Rican drivers are pretty crazy behind the wheel, so be alert. When driving on the freeways (called *autopistas*), particularly Route 52 from San Juan to Ponce, the left lane is often much smoother, as trucks don't drive on it. Actually, the left lane often seems to be the de facto travel lane and the right the passing lane. However, cars pass on both left and right, depending on what is open. In addition, don't be confused when you see highway mileage signs in kilometers and speed signs in miles. Finally, Puerto Rico is the land of more than a million cars—too many for the current infrastructure. It often seems that everyone who owns a car here is on the road at the same time, especially in the cities. Due to the effects of traffic lights on multi-lane roads, there are often traffic jams on secondary roads. East of San Juan, on Route 3, traffic can be heavy all the way to Fajardo. Traffic on roads around Ponce (Routes 1 and 2) can also jam up, although a bypass road has alleviated that problem a bit. Of course all major roads in and around San Juan will be very busy during rush hours, so plan accordingly. Be sure to ask your rental-car company for road sign translations (most are in Spanish) or bring your own Spanish-English dictionary.

Focus on Puerto Rico:
San Juan—The Long Weekend Destination

Where to go for a long or extended weekend in the sun? South Beach, in Miami? Forget it! That place is so ten years ago. The rest of Florida? Nah, it's just not very exotic or exciting. Havana is not yet easily accessible and is technically off-limits to Americans, a quick jaunt there isn't either easy or convenient. Where, then, does one go for a quick tropical getaway? Well, we think it's a no-brainer. There aren't many other choices where the weather is guaranteed hot, the destination is easy to reach for weekends or more, and there are great choices of restaurants and nightlife. Now the in-the-know are heading to San Juan.

What used to be San Juan's glittering and main tourist destination—the Condado area—while still a tad seedy is showing signs of a comeback. Anchored by the San Juan Marriott (the old Dupont

Plaza), the Condado resembles a cross between Waikiki and Miami Beach. There are some art deco buildings, lots of high-rises, hotel rooms, and a nice beach here. The water is clean and there is surf, so it's fun; and then there are the restaurants and nightlife. Old San Juan, home of some of the Caribbean's most valuable Spanish colonial architecture, has also experienced a boom, primarily due to the thriving cruise ship industry. While not directly on the beach (but on a rocky point at the entrance to the harbor), this pretty part of the city has some very cool places to stay. There is Ocean Park, east of the Condado, with the city's best beach and a string of charming and cheap guest houses. At the eastern end of the city and very near the airport, is Isla Verde, where most of San Juan's big and luxury properties are located.

San Juan is reasonably priced (especially with package deals) and now on a par with South Beach (the latter's prices have escalated dramatically in the last few years). And while you can go to Miami and taste its nightlife, restaurants, and beaches, here you get all that and you're *in the tropics,* too. You won't experience a chilling winter cold front in Puerto Rico. The weather is pretty much the same year-round (like Florida, summer gets more rain), and the summer in San Juan is actually much cooler than Florida because of the trade winds. Another bonus is that you can drive an hour out of San Juan and be in the mountains, or two hours and be in a beautiful Caribbean beach town. In Miami, where do you go for diversion—Ocala? Finally, Puerto Rico is 100 percent Latin, not semi-Latin like Miami.

Besides nightlife and beaches, San Juan also has lots of historical sights to see, almost all of them in Old San Juan. You could easily spend at least a half-day exploring or just hanging out in this beautifully restored part of the city. Not to be missed are **Fuerte San Felipe del Morro (El Morro)**, 787-729-6960, Calle del Morro, open daily from 9 A.M. to 5 P.M., English tours at 10 A.M. and 3 P.M., admission $2, children under 12 go free; **Casa Blanca,** 787-724-1454, open daily from 8 A.M. to 5 P.M., admission $2 adults, $1 seniors; **Catedral de San Juan,** 787-722-0861, open daily from 8 A.M. to 4 P.M. (it houses the remains of Ponce de León); **Iglesia San José,** 787-725-7501, open daily 8:30 A.M to 4 P.M., Sunday Mass at noon; **Museo Pablo Casals,** 787-723-9185, open Tuesday through

Saturday from 9:30 A.M. to 5:30 P.M., $1; **Museo de Arte e Historia,** 787-724-1875, open Tuesdays through Sundays from 10. A.M. to 4 P.M.; **Plaza de Armas** (the main square of Old San Juan, where San Juan's city hall has been located since 1789); and **La Forteleza** (which has been the governor's mansion since 1540), 787-721-7000, open Monday through Friday (except holidays) from 9 A.M. to 3:30 P.M., tours in English on the hour. There's a lot more to see—the above are just highlights. Stop in at **La Casita,** open Monday through Wednesday from 8:30 A.M. to 8 P.M., Thursday and Friday until 5:30 P.M., weekends from 9 A.M. to 8 P.M., 787-722-1709. Located on the Plaza de la Dársena by the cruise-ship docks, it's operated by the Puerto Rican Tourism Company and has a wealth of information, walking tours, and maps available.

Where to Stay: San Juan

¡*Caramba!* There are so many hotels, inns, resorts, guest houses, and *paradores* on Puerto Rico that the choices are staggering. However, with some weeding and sifting, which is our job, here are some suggestions. Most of the accommodations are in San Juan, but there are certainly great alternatives like Dorado, Rincón, Guánica, and Boquerón.

The Puerto Rico Tourism Company operates *Paradores Puertorriqueños*, a grouping of small hotels and inns scattered about the island, often in great locations. Don't expect cute little Vermont-style B&Bs or inns. The *paradores* are simple, motelish accommodations that are well under $100 a night and clean. Some are in the mountains, some are on or near a beach, but they all provide an inexpensive and comfy place to hang your hat while you explore the island. All have basic amenities, like air conditioning, TV, and phones, and many have pools. For a complete listing, www.gotopuertorico.com or call 800-866-7827, 787-721-2400 (in San Juan).

There are four different parts of San Juan in which you can stay. The primary area is **Isla Verde,** a newer big-hotel strip near the airport. This is where most of the large hotels are located. We recommend against staying in Isla Verde if the roar of jets landing and taking off will bother you (it is especially loud once you're east of the El San Juan). Another major area is the more centrally located

Condado, once the primary place for hotels and experiencing a renaissance of sorts. Between the Condado and Isla Verde is **Ocean Park.** This is a personal favorite as it's a residential neighborhood of charming two-story homes and some big old stucco houses on the beach. The beach itself is the best in the city (and a pretty beach in its own right). Accommodations here are guest houses, which are casual, relaxed, beachy, and cheap. We like this combination. The last area is **Old San Juan,** which is full of colonial architecture and character, although it is inconvenient to nightlife and the beach (everything is a cab ride away), and during the day the cruiseship–tourbus circuit swarms the area. Still, it's unique, and the two places we recommend there, El Convento and the Gallery Inn, are superb.

With all that in mind, here are our favorites:

Condado

San Juan Marriott Resort & Stellaris Casino, 1309 Ashford Avenue, San Juan, PR 00907. Stateside and Canada: 800-464-5005. Local: 787-722-7000, fax 787-722-6800.
Web site: www.marriott.com

Without a doubt, this is our favorite place to stay in the Condado. As a matter of fact, we prefer the Marriott to all the big hotels in San Juan. Its location is perfect, the beach in front is wide and spacious, the pool area is comfortable and private, the staff is friendly and helpful, and the lobby bar is a magnet for good musical talent and *Sanjuaneros* out for a dressy good time. Best of all, the size of the hotel doesn't overwhelm, and travel time from pool to room is less than five minutes—a major convenience. We also appreciate the fact that Marriott was key in the renaissance of this part of the Condado, renovating the old Dupont Plaza (closed in 1987 after a tragic fire), putting millions into the 21-story building and compact grounds, and reopening in 1995.

Modeled after a big-city hotel, there are 525 rooms, 17 suites, and an Executive Floor. Rooms are comfortable and tasteful, with details like two-line speaker phones, data ports, voice mail, safe, and even an iron and ironing board. We have our own spiritual beliefs and guide, so we find the replacement of the standard Gideon's Bible in the bedside table with that of the Church of Latter-Day

Saints (Marriott is based in Utah) to be a bit pushy. However, our bed was firm and the air conditioning worked well. The baths are a tad small, but the hotel was built in the days when bathrooms weren't meant to be lounges. All rooms have a lanai. If you get an oceanfront room, the sound of the surf will fill your room, even up to the 20th floor. We like the 24-hour room service, too. After a night on the town, we need something to absorb the alcohol.

Because the Marriott is centrally located, you can walk almost everywhere (except Old San Juan). Even the best nightclubs are an easy walk or cab ride (recommended) away. The resort has a spa, an excellent small gym, two lighted tennis courts, and the Stellaris Casino (which is fortunately located to the side of the lobby and thus not too intrusive).

Rates are *Ridiculous* and up (EP). However, corporate rates and package deals can reduce the bill by 30 percent or more.

Caribe Hilton, Calle Los Rosales, San Gerónimo Grounds, P.O. Box 9021872, San Juan, PR 00902-1872. Stateside and Canada: 800-468-8585. Local: 787-721-0303, fax 787-725-8849.

Opened in 1949, the Caribe Hilton is an institution on the island and is a focal point of activity in the city. Business, government, and cultural meetings and events happen here regularly. The hotel was extensively renovated in 1999, with a total redesign of the lobby and public areas, a new swimming complex, and a huge health club. Sitting in the breezy lobby of the hotel, you will see people from all walks of life and from everywhere—always a hubbub of activity. The hotel is the biggest in San Juan and a huge property for being in the midst of a city. Nestled on 17 acres on the other end of the Condado Bridge in an area called Puerto de Tierra; it consists of two multistory buildings and a tower, all of which house 645 rooms and suites (it's a big hotel). There are gardens with fish ponds, a new pool area centering the airy Terrace Bar (where the piña colada was invented in 1957), and the beach, which is man-made but still attractive and protected by a lagoon. On the grounds are three lighted tennis courts and a new health club and spa. The gym is the largest we've seen at a hotel, period. The size of a school gymnasium, it features lots of free weights, machines, treadmills, and a stadium ceiling. The spa with sauna and Jacuzzi costs extra.

There is also a small snack bar. Water sports can be arranged by the hotel. The recently redone rooms are a mix of pastel and dark green, with wall-to-wall carpeting and marble baths. Most rooms have lanais and all the amenities you would expect from a major international hotel. There are five restaurants, two bars, and a newly renovated casino. We love the fact that the hotel often has great Latin bands at the Oasis Bar, which has always been well attended by dressed-up locals. Also available is the Executive Business Center, which is free for use by hotel guests. For a fee, it will also provide secretarial and translation services, fax and photocopy service, and the use of PCs, with high-speed Internet, and binding.

Rates are *Wicked Pricey* and up (EP). Check for corporate rates or package deals.

Condado Plaza Hotel & Casino, 999 Ashford Avenue, P.O. Box 1270, San Juan, PR 00902. Stateside: 800-468-8588. Local: 787-721-1000, fax 787-722-7955.
Web site: www.condadoplaza.com
e-mail: buscen@prtc.net

The Condado Plaza is another large hotel (575 rooms and suites) and is on the other side of the bridge from the Caribe Hilton. Although it doesn't have an impressive lobby, it does have a fairly airy manageable casino with windows, so you know when the sun is coming up and when it's time for bed. The best thing about the hotel is the spacious and fun pool area (there are three declared pools—one is saltwater). The hotel shares a small, calm public beach anchoring one end of the bridge that spans the lagoon. They spent $40 million for a refurbishing in 1998, which was needed. Rooms are attractive and comfortably furnished and have all the standard amenities, including 24-hour room service and an iron and ironing board. The hotel consists of two buildings connected by a bridge over the road (we prefer the oceanside one). There are six very different restaurants and the La Fiesta Lounge, which has live Latin bands (we like that). There are two lighted tennis courts, a water sports complex offering kayaks and windsurfing (extra charge), and a fitness center with sauna and steam (extra charge).

Rates are *Wicked Pricey* (EP). Look for package deals.

Normandie Hotel, Riviera Avenue at the New Millennium Park, Call Box 50059, San Juan, PR 00902. Stateside and Canada: 877-987-2929. Local: 787-729-2929, fax 787-729-3083.
Web site: www.normandiepr.com

The 177-room Normandie was severely damaged by 1998's Hurricane Georges and reopened in January 2000. Located next to the Caribe Hilton complex and on a slice of beach, this is San Juan's only real art deco hotel. It looks like it's right out of South Beach. Architecturally, it's very interesting on the outside. The new lobby is on the small side, giving the hotel the feeling of being a small inn. The decor, however, while warm, isn't carried out throughout the hotel. There is a large atrium inside with the usual glass elevator and a restaurant and bar. But the place screams for a decorator and some foliage. The redecorated rooms are more a melange than art deco. We want to warm this place up. The pool is small, missing landscaping (you must walk from the hotel across the asphalt driveway to reach it—a missed opportunity). Management says the pool is slated to be renovated. The Jacuzzi, however, is no longer open. There is a small beach, but seriously folks, if you want art deco, go to South Beach.

Rates are *Very Pricey* (EP).

Best Western Hotel Pierre, Calle De Diego No. 105, Santurce, San Juan, PR 00914. Stateside: 800-528-1234. Local: 787-721-1200, fax 787-721-3118.
Web site: www.bestwestern.com

While it's not anywhere close to the beach (although it's only a 10-minute walk), the Hotel Pierre is a very attractive property and an excellent value for a full-service hotel in the Condado area. It's very popular with the business set, which is always a good sign. The recently renovated lobby features marble floors and plenty of places to sit, chat on your cell phone, and plan your day or evening. There's even a small gym with sauna. The hallways have been renovated with attractive drop ceilings of wooden slats, and the 184 rooms are undergoing a complete face-lift that will include new bathrooms and refrigerators and microwave ovens. All rooms have air conditioning, phones, and cable TV. There are three restaurants, a bar, and a pool on the grounds.

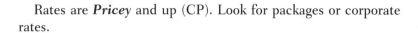

Rates are **Pricey** and up (CP). Look for packages or corporate rates.

Atlantic Beach Hotel, Calle Vendig No. 1, Condado, San Juan, PR 00907. Local: 787-721-6900, fax 787-721-6917.
Web site: www.atlanticbeachhotel.com
e-mail: reservations@atlanticbeachhotel.net

This is the Condado's gay hotel and the site of daily afternoon happy hour (4 to 6 P.M.) that is popular with both tourists and locals. This place needs not only a face-lift, but some lipo and major tucking, too. To quote the late great Bette Davis, "What a dump!" If you want to stay in a gay-friendly environment, stay at one of the guest houses in Ocean Park (see below). The bar, however, is definitely fun for happy hour, especially on Sundays. There is a restaurant adjoining the bar. Given the orientation of the hotel's guests, the beach in front is Condado's gay beach (the hotel provides chaises).

Rates are **Not So Cheap** (EP).

Isla Verde

Isla Verde is a strip of large condos and hotels on the beach side and every conceivable fast-food joint known to man on the other. The beach here is nice, and some people seem to love staying in this part of San Juan. Our biggest gripe is that the airport is down the street, and we loathe the sound of screaming jet engines while we're reading Jane Austen (very incongruous, indeed!). Incredibly, hotel chains keep building here, including the fairly new Ritz Carlton, which is literally across the street from the end of the runway where the jumbo jets rev their engines to take off. Hello? Anybody home? Fortunately, the El San Juan and the San Juan Grand (née The Sands), are far enough away so that the noise is only a dull roar. We also find it rather removed from the nightlife and restaurant scene, as a car or significant taxi ride is necessary. But the airport is close...

The Water Club, 2 Tartak Street, Isla Verde, PR 00979. Stateside: 888-265-6699. Local: 787-728-3610.
Web site: www.waterclubsanjuan.com

The of-the-moment accommodation in Puerto Rico—perhaps in all of the Caribbean—is this revamping of the Old Colonial San Juan Hotel, remained the Water Club when it debuted in late 2001. The intent was to create an ambiance that has more in common with a Manhattan boutique hotel than with a typical beach resort. Although it sits across the street from a good beach, the focus is on the modern, *Wallpaper* worthy interiors—no generic tropical print bedspreads here.

Falling water is a key element of the concept: there's a waterfall over corrugated metal behind the main bar, glass-enclosed waterfalls tumble inside the elevators (quite a head rush when the elevator zips up and down), and a hall mirror on each floor is drizzled with trickling water. The central lighting scheme throughout is dark and neon blue—votive candles glow in the lobby and hallways 24/7. By day, rooms are stylish and bright, with blond wood floors (faux, but attractive), and king-size beds angled toward the water; all rooms have at least a partial ocean view. All of the courant furnishings were designed to order. The sexy final concept for the bathrooms (not yet in place when we visited) includes double head showers with glass doors and stainless steel pedestal sinks. There are special touches like the CD and TV stand on a floor-to-ceiling swivel, the psychedelic blue glow that emanates from each room at night, and the "desires" board—a glass note pad and pen for guests to make maid requests on. There are a few annoyances: rooms don't have a real closet, just a recess in the wall with a hanger and, at the prices charged here, isn't collecting a rental fee for the front desk's library of CDs a little much?

There is a tiny rooftop pool, where Sunday afternoon champagne parties will be staged, and a bar with a terrific view just below with sushi and a fireplace. On the ground floor is another bar, while the second-floor restaurant, Tangerine, breaks with the blue light intrigue—the small dining room is all white with a single orange chair at each table (a tad too *de trop* for us). Room service is 24 hours, and the food is delicious, if somewhat skimpy in the portion department. The Water Club is located about a half-mile west of El San Juan, on a dead-end street that becomes jammed with traffic on Friday and Saturday nights. Yes, San

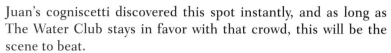

Juan's cogniscetti discovered this spot instantly, and as long as The Water Club stays in favor with that crowd, this will be the scene to beat.

Rates are **Wicked Pricey** (EP).

Wyndham El San Juan Hotel & Casino, 6063 Avenida Isla Verde, P.O. Box 9022872, San Juan, PR 00902-2872. Stateside and Canada: 800-468-3818. Local: 787-791-1000, fax 787-791-0390.
Web site: www.wyndham.com

The El San Juan, now a Wyndham resort, is the largest deluxe hotel-resort-casino property in Isla Verde—with 385 rooms and 21 suites on more than 15 acres. Its entrance—through a dim carved-mahogany lobby with a massive crystal chandelier hovering over the bar like the cloud shadow in a Magritte painting—is impressively different than most tropical hotels. The floors are dark marble. To the right is the best looking and most spacious casino in San Juan. To the left is the reception area, and beyond it the pools and beach. The outside area is fantastic. There are several pools, including a nice size lap pool and the requisite resort pool with waterfalls, islands, etc. Around it are a Jacuzzi and some very comfortable chaises with cushions (which we love). Pool bars seem to be everywhere, and overall it is a very attractive setting. There are ocean premier suites (*casitas*), which can be rented, that border one of the best big-hotel beaches in San Juan. Two lighted tennis courts and water sports round out the outdoor activities. Rooms are decorated in shades of yellow and green and have dark wood colonial-style furnishings. While on the smallish side, they are fully loaded, including such items as VCR, stereo, a tiny TV in the bathroom, tiled bath, an iron and ironing board, a hair dryer, and three phones. A new three-story structure on the grounds houses 21 luxury suites with the same amenities but with more space and privacy. On the roof of the main building is the Rooftop Spa and Fitness Center with steam and sauna. Downstairs there are seven dinner restaurants, two snack bars, eight cocktail lounges (including the Tequila Bar on the tenth floor and a cigar bar), and the Babylon disco (a dressy club where locals take their dates to impress them).

Rates are **Wicked Pricey** and up (EP). Look for packages.

Inter-Continental San Juan Resort & Casino, Avenida Isla Verde #5961, Isla Verde, San Juan, PR 00979 (mailing address: Box 6676, Loíza Station, Santurce, PR 00914-6676). Stateside and Canada: 800-443-2009. Local: 787-791-6100, fax 787-791-7091.
Web site: www.interconti.com
e-mail: sanjuan@interconti.com

Formerly the San Juan Grand, the Inter-Continental San Juan received a $15 million face-lift when it was the San Juan Grand, and its rooms and halls are undergoing renovation by its new owner, Inter-Continental. It still has that fabulous early '60s look—but now is yellow instead of white. The lobby's marble floors are more colorful now, and the mirror-and-chrome motif is gone. There is a good-size casino; when we were there, someone was gambling away thousands of dollars at the craps table (and enjoying every minute, strangely enough). Outside, there is a large free-form pool (reportedly the largest free-form pool in the Caribbean with Jacuzzi and swim-up bar) with the standard tropical resort feature of an island in the middle with bridges. There is a spacious beach in front with chaises. The rooms all have little lanais with soundproof sliders. The new décor features modern furnishings, gold-tone carpeting, yellow walls, artwork with dark woodwork, and a distinctly international or European feel. The renovated hallways feature dark mahogany woodwork and gold striated wallpaper. There are also five well-frequented restaurants on the premises, including Ruth's Chris Steak House (San Juan's best steak house).

Rates are **Wicked Pricey** and up (EP). Look for packages.

The Ritz Carlton San Juan Hotel & Casino, 6961 Avenue of the Governors, Isla Verde, Carolina, PR 00979. Stateside and Canada: 800-241-3333. Local: 787-253-1700, fax 787-253-0777.
Web site: www.ritzcarlton.com

While it is a Ritz—down to the crystal chandeliers, oriental rugs, dark heavy furniture (which we found rather out of place in tropical Puerto Rico), afternoon tea, and its renowned service—we couldn't grasp why they would build this resort (opened in 1997) adjacent to the runway of the international airport. The noise, especially on the entrance side, is horrendous when the jumbo jets rev their engines to take off. Even on the ocean side, where the very pretty and well-designed pool area is located, the roar of the jets could be heard through our iPod headphones (we were playing Destiny's Child—Joni Mitchell couldn't compete with the planes). The windows of the 414-room hotel are double-paned for noise insulation and do not open. There are only 21 lanais available, and they are on the ocean side. Our room was on the airport side, and we heard what sounded like muffed screams every time a plane took off. If this will bother you (as it did us), then look elsewhere.

Otherwise, this is a fine hotel, and it features the largest casino in Puerto Rico. All the amenities that make the Ritz famous are available, including twice-daily maid service and those sumptuous terry bathrobes. There is 24-hour room service, served with silver and china on a wheeled-in table—wonderful to enjoy while wearing those robes, a Ritz experience. Our standard room was on the smallish side, with dark wall-to-wall carpeting, mahogany furniture, and brightly colored upholstery. The baths are a symphony of marble.

Besides the pool (between jets) and the robes, we loved the Ritz's spa and fitness center, contained in a wing of the hotel. A 12,000-square-foot space, the gym is one of the best of any hotel on the island and includes a fabulous aerobics room with nine spinners, treadmills, and stationary bikes. All kinds of body pampering is available, as well as fitness and aerobics classes. There are two lighted tennis courts, a pretty beach in front, and all kinds of water sports available through the hotel. There are three restaurants, two bars, and the only casino in the Ritz chain.

Rates are **Wicked Pricey** and up (EP). Check for corporate rates or packages.

Ocean Park

This is a wonderful residential neighborhood without high-rise hotels and with the best beach in San Juan. There are several guest houses, four of which we recommend. All are mixed gay and straight, with the Ocean Walk and L'Habitation Beach Guest House being the gayest. But everyone of any persuasion is welcome at all four.

Numero Uno on the Beach, Calle Santa Ana No. 1, Ocean Park, Santurce, PR 00911. Local: 787-726-5010, fax 787-727-5482.

Numero Uno is one of our favorite places to stay in Puerto Rico and the best accommodation of its kind in San Juan. Located on the beach about halfway between Hostería del Mar and the Ocean Walk, this 11-room, two suite, three-story guest house is beautifully relaxed, friendly, and comfortable. Owners-managers Chris and Ester Laube (ex–New Jerseyans: he's American and she's Puerto Rican) know their business well, having completely renovated a dilapidated old house on the beach and built it into a solid business of repeat customers, all in a decade. Like all other guest houses in Ocean Park, the clientele here is mixed straight and gay, American and European. Numero Uno's restaurant, Pamela's, is one of the best in San Juan.

There are 12 comfortable, clean rooms, all with air conditioning, double or king-size beds, white-tiled floors, private baths, and no TVs. The downstairs has a plunge pool, and lots of shady places to sit and sip a cocktail while you reread *Valley of the Dolls*. The beach in front is never crowded and is sort of the gay section of the beach. Numero Uno provides chaises and beach towels for its guests.

Rates are *Not So Cheap* and up (CP).

Hostería del Mar, Calle Tapia No. 1, Ocean Park, Santurce, PR 00911. Stateside: 877-727-3302, Local: 787-727-3302, fax 787-268-0772.
Web site: netdial.caribe.net/~hosteria
e-mail: hosteria@caribe.net

Situated right on the beach, there is a very tranquil air at Hostería del Mar, apparent as you enter through a gate, pass a goldfish pool, and step into a breezy lounge attractively decorated in light woods, rattans, and tropical plants. To your left is one of our favorite places to have lunch in San Juan (see "Where to Eat"). The restaurant's setting is extraordinary, especially since it's in a city. Sitting inside you defiinitely wouldn't know you were in San Juan—the sound of the surf is omnipresent. The 23 rooms are simply but nicely decorated, with terra-cotta-tiled floors, rattan furnishings, air conditioning, cable TV, phones, and private baths. Many have lanais and ocean views, and some have kitchenettes. The beach out front is never crowded.

Rates are *Cheap* and up (EP).

L'Habitation Beach Guest House, Calle Italia No. 1957, Ocean Park, Santurce, PR 00911. Local: 787-727-2499, fax 787-727-2599. Web site: www.habitationbeach.webjump.com e-mail: habitationbeach@msn.com

This 10-room gay guest house sits next door to Numero Uno and is now owned by Marie and Michel Barrabes. Known years ago as the Beach House, L'Habitation Beach Guest House is a simple and casual place to stay, with a sand patio and bar in front for guests. We hope the owners will make good on their promise to give this hotel a spiffing up, as it's looking a "bit long in the tooth." The patio furniture, cement deck, and hotel exterior cry out for a fresh coat of paint. Rooms are basic, clean but comfortable, although some new and fluffy towels and pillows would be welcome. But the price is right, so don't expect too much. All rooms have ceiling fans, air conditioning, and private baths, but no room phones. The best and most spacious rooms front the beach (ask for room 8 or 9). Windows are louvered—there is no glass.

The beach bar serves burgers and sandwiches for lunch. A complimentary Continental breakfast is also served at the beach bar. The guest house provides chaises for its guests. People with children are discouraged from staying at L'Habitation Beach.

Rates are *Cheap* (CP).

Old San Juan

Old San Juan now has more lodging possibilities, partly due to the cruise-ship impact on this part of the city, but also due to the beautiful Spanish colonial architecture of the oldest part of the city. Two small hotels, the fabulous El Convento and the art-filled Gallery Inn, are great choices for those seeking something different. The Wyndham Old San Juan is a larger chain hotel that caters to the cruise-ship industry. While there is no beach in Old San Juan (the closest one is in the Condado), it is surrounded by water on three sides. Water views abound from rooftops, from between buildings, and from the steep, narrow streets.

Hotel El Convento, Calle Cristo No. 100, Old San Juan, PR 00902. Stateside and Canada: 800-468-2779. Local: 787-723-9020, fax 787-721-2877.

Web site: www.elconvento.com

e:mail: elconvento@aol.com

Probably the finest small hotel in San Juan (it's the only "Small Luxury Hotels of the World" member property in Puerto Rico), the 58-room El Convento resides in a 350-year old building across from the Cathedral of Old San Juan. Occupied for 250 years by Carmelite nuns, the building was abandoned in 1903 due to neglect. Many uses followed, until it was finally purchased in 1995 and experienced a much-needed $16 million face-lift, completed in 1997 and fully utilizing the architectural distinctiveness of the building and its stunning multistoried, arched interior courtyard.

We loved the whole ambiance, look, and energy of this place (maybe all that past praying rubbed off on us a little). The courtyard features several restaurants, including El Picoteo Tapas Bar—the best place for drinks in Old San Juan. (Be careful with the olives in your martini. Savoring that final martini treat, we bit down to discover that it wasn't pitted and consequently cracked a crown. Now *that* was an expensive drink!) The courtyard also has a shopping arcade on the ground level.

The hotel occupies the top four floors of the building (the lobby is located on the third floor). Access is controlled by an elevator passkey (to keep out the riffraff). Guests are met by a porter at the front gate and are escorted to the reception desk. The rooms are all different, in both size and décor. Standard rooms are on the small side—an upgrade may be desired. Walls are brightly colored and hand-painted. The furniture is a mélange of restored mahogany antiques and hand-crafted wrought-iron pieces. All rooms are air conditioned and have CD-stereo systems, TV-VCRs, two-line phones, data ports, fridges, irons and ironing boards, and bathrobes. El Convento also has suites, including the spectacular and intriguing Gloria Vanderbuilt Suite, with marble floors, parlor, hand-painted and -stenciled walls, Spanish colonial antiques, high beamed ceilings painted blue, vintage art, and black marble bath with Jacuzzi—all for $1,200 a day. There is a new fitness center with treadmills and free weights, a small pool, and a Jacuzzi on a terrace with fab views of the Fortaleza, the Cathedral, and the harbor.

Rates are **Wicked Pricey** and up (CP). Look for packages.

The Gallery Inn, Calle Norzagaray No. 204, Old San Juan, PR
00901. Local: 787-722-1808, fax 787-977-3929.
Web site: www.thegalleryinn.com
e-mail: reservations@thegalleryinn.com

Now *this* is an unusual place. Packed floor to ceiling with the art
of Jan D'Esopo (mostly watercolors and sculptures), the Gallery
Inn has an ambiance of a small museum. Indeed, the inn's lobby
could easily be mistaken for a cramped art gallery (we weren't even
sure we were in the right place). However, the lobby leads to an
inner courtyard and working studio with a more comfortable sense
of space. We were fascinated by the artwork which, after a while,
made us a tad dizzy from constantly changing focus. Seated with a
cocktail, we regained our composure.

Set in a rambling 350-year-old building at the crest of Old San
Juan, this inn has become a popular gathering spot for the young,
up-and-coming bohemian crowd. The views from the Inn's roof terrace, called the Wine Deck, are breathtaking. Begun in 1984, the
Inn has grown over time, and the rooms reflect the owners' constant collecting of interesting furnishings and art. There are many
quiet nooks, crannies, patios, and gardens for repose or reading.
There's even an air-conditioned music room with a Steinway grand
piano for the pianists among us. Several caged birds also live here,
as do the owners, Jan D'Esopo and Manuco Gandía. Twenty-two
suites and rooms, primarily named after children and grandchil-
dren of Jan and Manuco, are scattered throughout the Inn. All are
individually decorated, have phones (no TVs), and all have private
baths and air conditioning.

Rates are *Very Pricey* and up (CP).

Wyndham Old San Juan Hotel & Casino, 100 Brumbaugh, Old
San Juan, PR 00901. Stateside and Canada: 800-WYNDHAM.
Local: 787-721-5100, fax 787-721-1111.
Web site: www.wyndham.com

With four major hotels and more than 1,800 rooms and suites in
Puerto Rico, Texas-based Wyndham Hotels and Resorts is now the
biggest hotel chain on the island. The Wyndham Old San Juan is its
smallest property, with 240 rooms in a nine-story building opposite

the cruise-ship terminal. Opened in 1997, the hotel gets most of its business from cruiseship customers who stay at the beginning or end of their trips. The hotel has a very small lobby that is dominated by the cacophony of slot machine bells from the adjoining casino. Fleeing that, the guest rooms are accessed through rather drab, dreary, and cut-up halls. Deluxe rooms face outside and have stucco walls, blond wood furnishings, wall-to-wall carpeting, and earth-tone fabrics—which were a refreshing change from the omnipresent pastels. We found the rooms and windows smallish, but the baths were comfortable, with good shower heads and Italian tiles. Other amenities include two-line speakerphones with data ports and voicemail, a safe, satellite TV, and an iron and ironing board. We also liked that feather pillows were available as well as 24-hour room service. There is a small rooftop pool with tiled deck and a great view of the harbor. A tiny fitness center is adjacent.

Rates are **Very Pricey** and up (EP). Look for packages or corporate rates.

Where to Eat

San Juan is a big city and there are restaurants galore—from very expensive *chichi* bistros to the little snack bar on the street. By all means leave your hotel and sample and experience. We've tried to weed through the myriad of choices and to provide a good cross-section of the San Juan dining scene. Old San Juan seems to be *the* happening place in dining and should definitely be explored. But other parts of the city also hold their own, so you will never be far from a good restaurant.

Keep in mind that all the large hotels and resorts now have several restaurants offering a variety of international cuisine. While the food at many of these resorts is good, the one thing they all have in common is that they are very expensive and overpriced. Now, if you're at Dorado Beach, for example, which is a 45-minute drive from town, you may have to bite the bullet and eat at the resort for sheer convenience. However, if you're staying right in San Juan, why sit home? Set thee out and about!

Here are our suggestions:

Old San Juan

Amadeus, Calle San Sebastian No. 106, 722-8635. Serving all kinds of Puerto Rican and Caribbean cuisine, this very attractive restaurant in the heart of Old San Juan is a festive stop for lunch or dinner. We've had both good and bad meals here, but it is fun. Open till 1 A.M., midnight Sunday and Monday. Reservations are suggested. $$$

La Bombonera, Calle San Francisco No. 259, 722-0658. An institution in Old San Juan, this is a great place for cheap Puerto Rican food when you're in the historic district. It's packed at lunchtime. Reputed to have the best Puerto Rican coffee in town. Open daily from 7:30 A.M. until 8:30 P.M. $$

Café Berlin, Calle San Francisco No. 407, 722-5205. If you're looking for vegetarian or lighter and healthier fare, this is a fine and rather hip place for breakfast, lunch and dinner. It's not at all expensive, and the Caribbean and international fare includes great breads, salads, and desserts. If you just want coffee or herbal tea, this is it. $$

La Chaumiére, Calle Tetuán No. 367, 722-3330. If you want French-Provençal cuisine, this is San Juan's best. It's also one of San Juan's most elegant and most expensive restaurants. Closed Sundays. Reservations are advised. Dinner only. $$$$$

Chef Marisoll Creative Cuisine, Calle Cristo No. 202, 725-7454. Located in a ornate balconied courtyard, chef Marisoll, one of the few female chefs heading a major restaurant in Puerto Rico, offers a continental menu with Caribbean flourishes. Dining can be al fresco, if desired. Closed Mondays. Reservations suggested. Lunch and Dinner. $$$$

Dragonfly, 364 Fortaleza, Old San Juan, 977-3886. This hot new Asian eatery is across the street from the Parrot Club, and by the same entrpreneur, Robert Trevino. There are only seven tables, and no reservations are taken (expect a wait), although there's a community table option or you can dine at the bar. The room is painted deep red and appointed in assorted chinoiserie, the music is Buddha Bar, and the gorgeous waitresses wear long silk dresses, slit up the leg. It's got sex appeal to spare, but the food is also indelible: Peking duck nachos, quesadilla spring rolls, ceviche in coconut milk and ginger, and—well, you get the idea. Trevino will have yet another new restaurant and club opening on the corner just as this books comes out—sure to be another smash. $$$$

La Mallorquina, Calle San Justo No. 207, 722-3261. This is a fine old-style restaurant that serves Puerto Rican and Spanish specialties (try the *asopao*—a Puerto Rican rice dish). Set in an old building with murals and ceiling fans, this is a very pleasant place for lunch. This is San Juan's oldest restaurant and has been owned and operated by the same family since 1848. Popular at lunch. Closed Sundays. Lunch and Dinner. $$$

The Parrot Club, Calle Fortaleza No. 363, 725-7370. One of the hottest restaurants in town is chef Robert Trevino's Parrot Club, featuring *"nuevo latino"* cuisine—best described as a mélange of Puerto Rican and other Latin dishes. Colorful and lively, the restaurant and its popular bar are always packed.

Il Perugino, Calle Cristo No. 105, 722-5481. Old San Juan's best Italian cuisine is served in this old colonial building. Specialties include homemade pastas and a superb wine cellar. Closed Sunday. Dinner only. $$$$

El Picoteo, Hotel El Convento, Calle Cristo No. 100, 643-1597. The best place for drinks in Old San Juan, El Picoteo serves tapas and light fare and is a symphony of connecting arches and tones of burnt sienna. Closed Mondays. Lunch and Dinner. $$

Yukiyú, Calle Recinto Sur No. 311, 722-1423 and 721-0653. With a great sushi bar in a comfortable setting, Yukiyú also offers teppan naki and other Japanese fare. Lunch and Dinner. $$$

Condado

Ajili Mójili, 1052 Ashford Avenue, 725-9195. This is the best place in San Juan to sample authentic Puerto Rican cuisine. The restaurant, in a new, larger location, is very attractive and full of locals, so you know it's good. Great service, too. Try the *mofongo* (made with mashed green plantains, garlic and pork rinds and stuffed with meat or seafood). Open for lunch and dinner (on Saturdays for dinner only). Reservations are suggested. $$$

Cherry Blossom, 1309 Ashford Avenue, 723-7300. Part of the San Juan Marriott Resort, this Japanese steak and seafood restaurant is quite good and has an excellent sushi bar. $$$$

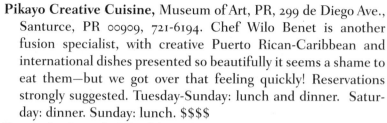

Pikayo Creative Cuisine, Museum of Art, PR, 299 de Diego Ave., Santurce, PR 00909, 721-6194. Chef Wilo Benet is another fusion specialist, with creative Puerto Rican-Caribbean and international dishes presented so beautifully it seems a shame to eat them—but we got over that feeling quickly! Reservations strongly suggested. Tuesday-Sunday: lunch and dinner. Saturday: dinner. Sunday: lunch. $$$$

Ramiro's, Avenida Magdalena No. 1106, 721-9049. Serving delicious international cuisine with Spanish-Castilian flourishes (dubbed "New Creole"), the Ramiro brothers create food that is as pretty to look at as it is good to eat. Closed for lunch on Saturday. Reservations are suggested. $$$$$

Vía Appia, 1350 Ashford Avenue, 725-8711. If you want Southern Italian cuisine (lasagna, baked ziti, spaghetti, eggplant parmesan, etc.) and pizza, this is a pleasant place to sit and eat under the awning in front. Although the service can be slow and at times indifferent, the food is hearty and the price is right. $$

Isla Verde

Pescadería Atlántica, Calle Loíza No. 2475, Punta Las Marías, 726-6654. In a new and bigger location, this is the place to go if you want really fresh seafood at reasonable prices. Popular with locals at lunch and dinner. Don't expect a fancy restaurant, just fresh fish. Closed Sunday. $$$

Ruth's Chris Steak House, Inter-Continental San Juan Resort and Casino, 791-6100. Even with such a difficult name to pronounce, Ruth's Chris is renowned as the best steak joint in the city. If you crave beef, this is the place. Dinner. $$$

Ocean Park

Hostería del Mar, Calle Tapia No. 1, 727-3302. One of the best spots for lunch in San Juan. You dine in a wooden pavilion with windows open to the beach and the trade winds. The service is lacking but the menu is rich, from macrobiotic and vegetarian to criollo and chicken and fish dishes. They also serve great sandwiches. It's good for dinner ($$$) lunch ($$) and breakfast ($).

Kasalta Bakery, Calle McLeary No. 1966, 727-7340. An institution in Ocean Park, this very popular local bakery and cafeteria eatery for breakfast, lunch, and dinner serves the best *café con leche* in town. The prices are really cheap here, too. Lunch and dinner specials include Puerto Rican dishes (*caldo gallego*, for instance) that are completely unknown to non-Latinos. Also popular are the Cuban sandwiches—a meal in themselves. Open daily from 6 A.M. till 10 P.M. A definite must stop! $

Pamela's Caribbean Cuisine, Numero Uno on the Beach, Calle Santa Ana No. 1, 726-5010. Executive chef Esteban Torres continues the excellent cuisine of this restaurant, which has created quite a stir in restaurant-rich San Juan. Pamela's also now has air conditioning, more space, and a view of the beach from every table (the wall to the beach has been opened up). Service may be a tad slow, but the fusion of Caribbean and international cuisine and the use of fresh island produce and seafood makes for a wonderful dining experience. *¡Sabroso!* Open daily for lunch (noon to 3 P.M.) and dinner (7 to 10:30 P.M.). Reservations suggested. $$$$

Ristorante Casa Di Legno, Calle María Moczo No. 57, 728-6440. A wonderful Italian restaurant in the old Mona's space. Chef Pierre St. Hubert has created one of San Juan's best-kept secrets, with more than 40 choices of pasta, seafood, and meat dishes. Closed Mondays. $$$$

Miramar

Augosto's Cuisine, Excelsior Hotel, Avenida Ponce de León No. 801, 725-7700. A favorite restaurant among well-to-do locals, Augosto's features one of the finest chefs on the island and offers an international menu in an elegant setting. Reservations suggested. $$$$

Chayote, Olimpo Court Hotel, Avenida Miramar No. 603, 722-9385. Consistently rated one of San Juan's best dining experiences. Chef Alfredo Ayala merges Caribbean, Puerto Rican, and international cuisine in such a delicious way that Chayote is the delight of in-the-know locals. Reservations a must. Closed Sundays and Mondays. Lunch and Dinner. $$$$

Puerto Nuevo

Aurorita's, Avenue De Diego No. 303, 783-2899. Good Mexican food, live mariachi music (Thursday through Sunday), and an out-of-the-way location (take a cab) make this a fun excursion. Closed Mondays. $$

Going Out

Get out those cha cha heels! With the best and greatest variety in the Caribbean, nightlife is why you stay in San Juan. There are lots of bars and clubs of all persuasions, and there is no set closing time. Most places close when the last person spins off the dance floor and stumbles into the street. As in any city, weekend nights will be the busiest and most crowded in the clubs. Also, all clubs will usually have a cover charge of between $5 and $15 (especially on weekends), which usually includes at least one free drink. And if you like to gamble, all the big hotels in Condado and Isla Verde have casinos (the most glittering is the one at the El San Juan in Isla Verde). So take your disco nap, strap on those sling backs or put on those Pradas, and off you go into the night.

Straight Bars and Clubs

The two hottest straight clubs in San Juan at the moment are Stargate and Club Lazer. But we've listed some other choices if you get tired of them and want a change of pace. Note that when going to the straight clubs here, people tend to get dressed up—that means no shorts, T-shirts, athletic shoes, or sandals for men (jeans are iffy; best to wear dressier pants); for women, dresses are preferred (the tighter and more leg showing, the better—remember, this is macho and sexist Latin America).

Asylum, Avenida Ponce de León No. 1420, Santurce, 723-3416. A dressy dance club that is popular with the local crowd. It's open Thursday through Saturday.

Bachus, Hyatt Regency Ceromar Beach Resort and Casino, Dorado, 787-796-1234. This newly established "mixed" club opened in 2000. It's open Thursday-Saturday, with Friday being the hottest night. The Club features a wide range of music with places to sit and get intimate.

Club Babylon, El San Juan Hotel, Isla Verde, 791-2781. This is dressy disco for good date impressions. This gets the Euro-trashy element as well as local flashy types. Open Thursday through Saturday. This is the most popular spot for singles.

Club Lazer, Calle Cruz No. 251, Old San Juan, 725-7581. This is San Juan's premier disco, located in the heart of Old San Juan. Here you'll hear all the current dance hits with all the high-tech accoutrements you expect in a hot club, plus there is a roof-deck garden jungle. It's stylish, it's fun, and it gets packed.

Dunbar's, Calle McLedary No. 1954, Ocean Park, 728-2920. This is a casual, popular bar in Ocean Park, packed with locals.

Houlihan's, 1309 Ashford Avenue, Condado, 723-8600. Always packed, somewhat dressy, and featuring live music on weekends. Just look for the line out front.

Parrot Club, Calle Fortaleza No. 363, Old San Juan, 729-8618. This restaurant gets very lively and crowded after the dinner crowd leaves (if they do). Open till 1 A.M.

Stargate, Avenida Roberto H. Todd No. 1, Santurce, 725-4664. Located just south of the Condado and the expressway, across the street from the fast-food plaza. The clientele here are mostly Puerto Rican young professionals, who are much more exciting and interesting than their American counterparts.

Gay and Lesbian Bars and Clubs

San Juan has the best, and pretty much only, gay and lesbian nightlife in the Caribbean. While there is a little nightlife scene in Santo Domingo in the Dominican Republic, San Juan is it until you get as far south as Caracas, Venezuela. Many of the "gay" clubs in Puerto Rico are both gay and lesbian mixed, especially outside of San Juan. And everyone, it seems, is dropping the "gay" and "straight" labels all together. You'll find many of "both" no matter where you go dancing in San Juan. Gay nights at straight clubs (which change constantly, so be sure to check) include Mondays at **Club Millennium**, Thursdays at **Club Lazer**, and Sundays at **Asylum**. And don't forget the daily happy hour at the **Atlantic Beach Hotel**. (Sundays are popular). Among the best clubs:

Cups at the Barn, Calle San Mateo No. 1708, Santurce, 268-3570. Where the girls are. Very popular on Wednesday and Friday and very busy.

Eros, Avenida Ponce de Leon No. 1257, Santurce, 722-1131. The hottest gay club in San Juan (and the best dance club in the city) is located next to the Metro Theater and just around the corner from Stargate. The dj spins world-class house, and there are often shows starting around 1 A.M. Many lesbian couples come here to dance, and you'll also see cool straight couples. Open Wednesday through Sunday.

Out on the island, Ponce has **The Cave** (no phone), Barrio Teneria No. 15. In San Germán, there's **Hacienda Villa Coqui,** 264-6103, Barrio Minillas, Carretera 102, Km. 38, open Friday and Sunday. Boquerón has a gay-friendly pub called **Yabadaba** (no phone), Road No. 110. Further east in Isabella is **Villa Ricomar** (no phone), Bario Jobas, Carretera No. 459, Sector la Sierra (enter in front of Brendy Pizza), open Friday through Sunday. For those staying in San Juan, try to get a Puerto Rican to take you to **Villa Caimito** for its very local Sunday afternoon and evening tea dance (they play salsa and merengue). It's located in the hills outside of Caguas and is impossible to find unless the driver has been there before. Finally, be sure to pick up a copy of *Puerto Rico Breeze* for local listings and events.

AROUND THE REST OF PUERTO RICO
(CLOCKWISE FROM SAN JUAN)

Where to Stay
The Northeast Coast
Río Grande and Río Mar

Located 19 traffic-prone miles east of San Juan's international airport and just west of the pretty and popular (with locals) Luquillo beaches are Río Grande and its Río Mar development. In this once sleepy part of Puerto Rico, the mid-1990s saw the rapid development of the 451-acre Río Mar Resort, swallowing up a mile of pristine beach with a big resort hotel, two golf courses, and condo developments. We weren't terribly impressed with the look and design of the resort. We think that the Dorado/Cerromar Beach resort is the gold standard which no other big island property has yet to successfully emulate (the Rockefellers had taste and vision when it came to creating resorts).

Río Mar is very close to El Yunque National Forest (see the "Don't Miss" section at the end of this chapter) and the Fajardo marina mecca on the east coast. Luquillo Beach is virtually next door and is a fun place to hang out and commune with *puertorriqueños*. Luquillo also has Puerto Rico's first wheelchair-accessible beach recreational facility. There is a ramp system from the parking lot right into the water, as well as wheelchair-accessible rest rooms. For more information on Luquillo wheelchair facilities, call Compania Parque Nacional at 787-622-5200

Westin Río Mar Beach Resort & Ocean Villas, 6000 Río Mar Boulevard, Río Grande, PR 00745. Stateside and Canada: 800-237-8129. Local: 787-888-6000, fax 787-888-6600.
Web site: www.westinriomar.com

The 600-room (and suite) Westin Río Mar Beach Resort & Casino sprawls along the beach in a very long, multistoried and rather architecturally bland building. Fifty-eight ocean villa suites were built next to the main hotel and opened in 2000. Popular for its convention facilities as well as its two Championship 18-hole golf courses (designed by the Fazio Brothers and Greg Norman) that spread out behind and around the hotel, we find this just another big, expensive, and boring place to stay. True, golfers and expense-accounters will love it, and there are a slew of other activities. These include 13 Har-Tru tennis courts (four lighted), a spa and fitness facility, water sports and dive center, three beachfront pools, kids' club, daily activities calendar, and (yawn) the requisite casino. Far more appealing to us is its proximity to El Yunque and San Juan (but we'd rather *stay* in San Juan—that's just our personal preference). The palm-lined beach is pretty but it can get a tad rough. The sand here is coarse, a light shade of brown (it is not a white-sand beach).

Things get better on the inside. The rooms are new and close to the sea. We like that oceanside guests can open their slider and hear the surf. The golf course side has very pretty views of the almost perpetually cloud-topped El Yunque summit and the mountains around it. The room décor is attractive and colorful. All have lanais, air conditioning, phones with voice mail, data port, and conference-calling ability, minibars and coffeemakers, TVs with in-room movies, Nintendo, video account review and checkout, and irons and ironing boards. We like that the Westin has 24- hour room service, since we'll be hungry after a night out in San Juan. The hotel also has a business center and several restaurant and bar possibilities.

Rates are **Ridiculous** and up (EP). Look for packages and corporate discounts.

Fajardo

The northeast corner of Puerto Rico has the huge Roosevelt Roads U.S. Naval Station, El Yunque National Forest, and the bustling town of Fajardo—a major marina area for boats due to its proximity to the marine playground of several Puerto Rican islands, cays, and the Virgin Islands. Fajardo is also where ferries and most scheduled air service depart for Culebra and Vieques. Due to traffic, the drive from San Juan can take an hour to an hour and a half. Just north of Fajardo, on the bluffs of Las Croabas, is the gigantic Wyndham El Conquistador Resort & Country Club.

Wyndham El Conquistador Resort & Country Club. 1000 El Conquistador Avenue, Fajardo, PR 00738. Stateside and Canada: 800-468-5228. Local: 787-863-1000, fax 787-863-6500.

Web site: www. wyndham.com

With over 500 acres, 919 rooms and suites, an acclaimed Arthur Hill 18-hole golf course, seven tennis courts (four lighted), six swimming pools, a marina, all kinds of water sports (including a dive shop), its own private island with beaches, two restaurants and bars, chaises, horseback riding, a fitness center, nine restaurants,

31

eight bars, shopping arcade, a casino, and even a funicular to climb part of the 300-foot bluff over which the hotel is sprawled, the Wyndham El Conquistador Resort & Country Club is the biggest hotel in Puerto Rico. Indeed, it can take 20 minutes just to walk from top to bottom. The hotel has four distinct guest wings or buildings. At the top of the hill is the La Vista Wing, midway down the hill is the Las Brisas Wing (where we stayed), and at the bottom of the hill near or on the water are Las Olas and La Marina Villages. Adjacent to the La Vista Wing is Las Casitas, which is not a Wyndham property (see below) and has 90 luxury villas with a price tag to match. The first Golden Door Spa in the Caribbean is also located there.

While it is a tad large for our taste (bigger isn't *always* better), El Conquistador will appeal to those who want a self-contained resort with lots of options and activities. Most of the hotel's activities are on the top of the hill, including the soaring lobby and the casino. Also on top is the striking main pool area featuring several levels, three pools (including a lap pool), columns, palm trees, and fab views. Those who want to be near them should consider staying in La Vista or Las Brisas. The yellow-toned décor of the rooms is quite nice and a refreshing change from pastels. All rooms have lanais, air conditioning, three multilined phones with voice mail, two TVs with movie channels and VCR, bars, safes, fridges, irons and ironing boards, and good-size baths. But what we really loved was the stereo system with three-disc CD and dual-cassette player—a rarity in any big resort.

We didn't like three things about the resort. We found the dining experience to be unexceptional and very expensive—even with nine choices. Given its location, going out to dine in Fajardo is inconvenient. We also did not like having to schlep to Palomino Island by scheduled water taxi (they leave every 30 minutes between 9 A.M. and 4 P.M.—the last taxi returns at 6 P.M.). It's bad enough just getting to the bottom of the hill! While exclusively used by hotel guests, the 100-acre island has a small swimming beach that can get crowded and had lots of seaweed in the water when we were there.

Rates are **Wicked Pricey** and up (EP). Look for packages and corporate discounts.

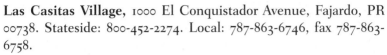

Las Casitas Village, 1000 El Conquistador Avenue, Fajardo, PR 00738. Stateside: 800-452-2274. Local: 787-863-6746, fax 787-863-6758.
Web site: www.wyndham.com

With prices starting at around $800 a night for a one-bedroom villa *without* a water view, we'd rather go to St. Barts—even if there *is* a personal butler who is assigned to each villa! There *are* limits. One of two "Five Diamond AAA Award" recipients in the Caribbean (the other is the Four Seasons on Nevis), Las Casitas has 90 one-, two-, and three-bedroom *casitas* and the Golden Door Spa. Designed to resemble a Spanish colonial village, the villas have a lot of the same amenities as its next-door neighbor, plus the afore-mentioned butler, 24-hour room service, private pool, fully equipped kitchen, and your favorite refreshments and reading materials stocked in your villa before you arrive. (No, they're not psychic and they don't have access to your supermarket scanner card records. The reservations people ask lots of questions.) Need-less to say, the villas are nicely done and quite luxurious. But you still have to take that damn water taxi to get to the beach!

Rates are ***Beyond Belief*** (CP). There are packages, but the rate category doesn't even come close to changing!

Naguabo

Casa Flamboyant B&B, P.O. Box 175, Naguabo, PR, 00718. Local: 787-874-6074 or 787-613-3454, fax 787-874-6135.
Web site: www.casaflamboyant.com (no e-mail!!)

Perched up in the mountains at the southern cusp of the El Yunque Rain Forest, this petite B&B (three rooms and a separate two-story villa (upstairs bedroom and downstairs living area with three daybeds and kitchen) sits on 25 lush and landscaped acres with over 200 kinds of trees, 50 species of orchids and over 100 exotic ferns. Nearby waterfalls of the Cubuy River provide natural ambi-ent sound. The tiled deck of the small but attractive and heated swimming pool has distant views of the Caribbean to the southeast. Even though this is a B&B, there are details and amenities of a lux-ury lodging, such as cotton sheets have a 350-thread count and a variety of massages on offer. The eclectic décor runs from pink and frilly with painted angelic statuary to more sedate yellow tones and wood paneling. One guest room and the villa have terraces and all rooms have private baths. Casa Flamboyant is off the beaten path (roughly between Fajardo and Palmas de Mar), and thus a good choice for those seeking peace and quiet. Activities, however, can be arrranged. There are several local-style seafood restaurants in Playa Punta Santiago (about a 20-minute drive down the mountain). No children under 12 allowed during the winter season.

Rates are *Not so Cheap* and up. Breakfast included.

The East Coast
Palmas del Mar

Located on the southeast coast near the town of Humacao on almost 2,800 acres, this is a condo-resort development of mammoth, sprawling, haphazard, and sometimes not-so-pretty proportions. Popular as a weekend haven for *sanjuaneros* (it's less than an hour from San Juan) and snowbirds from the North, Palmas del Mar boasts more than three miles of beaches (including one with lifeguards/bar/cafe), two eighteen-hole golf courses (designed by Gary Player and Rees Jones), 20 tennis courts (seven lighted), an equestrian center, seven pools, a fitness center, a large boat basin with several marinas and Coral Head Divers, the rather stark and behemoth Palmanova Plaza shopping center, more than 15 restaurants, cafes and pizza joints, several bars, and a casino. Candelero has a resort here and several of the condo clusters have all kinds of rental units available. Although we prefer other parts of Puerto Rico (Palmas is not our style), Palmas del Mar may be a good and affordable alternative for families who go the condo rental route. Contact Coldwell Banker or Diane Marsters (800-835-0199 or 787-850-3030, www.marstersrealty.com), Palmas del Mar Real Estate (787-852-8888), or RE/MAX de Palmas (787-850-7069).

Candelero Resort at Palmas del Mar, 170 Candelero Drive, P.O. Box 2020, Humacao, PR 00791. Stateside and Canada: 800-725-6273. Local: 787-852-6000, fax 787-852-6320.
Web site: www.palmasdelmar.com

We had issues with this 99-room, 81-villa resort within a resort. Upon arrival, we had to wait two hours for our room to be ready (and we arrived well after check-in time). The tile floor of our room was wet when we walked in, the air-conditioning unit barely worked and was noisy to boot, there weren't enough towels in the bathroom—and the management *knew* we were travel writers. The décor was rather minimalist tropical, but the room had cable TV, a coffeemaker, a hair dryer, and a safe. We were also very discouraged that there was no room service. Throwing our bags down, we left the room to let the floor dry and refresh ourselves in the pool. But the hotel's small pool was loaded with screaming kids (and babies!). There was no way we'd go in *that* water! We headed to the beach, which was crowded and filed with surfers right in the bathing area, which we thought a tad dangerous. We thought the general condition of the place needed attention, although we realize that Candelero had only recently taken over. Maybe things have improved, but we couldn't wait to leave not only the hotel but all of Palmas del Mar.

Rates are **Very Pricey** and up (EP). Look for packages and corporate discounts.

The South Coast
Ponce

Ponce is a wonderful mélange of Spanish and Caribbean architecture, with other styles thrown in for the hell of it. In downtown Ponce, the Spanish colonial influence is very pronounced. Most of the central district around **Plaza Las Delicias** has been or is in the process of being restored and is definitely worth seeing. In the plaza are the **Catedral Nuestra Señora de Guadalupe** and the very colorful **Parque de Bombas** which is closed for renovations until 2002. Other must stops while in Ponce are the **Museo de la Música Puertorriqueño**, 848-7016, corner of Calles Isabel and Salud, open Wednesday through Sunday, 8:30 A.M. to 4:30 P.M., which provides a great perspective on Puerto Rican music from *bomba* and *plena* to *danza* and *salsa*; the neoclassical and colorful facade of **Teatro la Perla** (Calle Mayor); the **Museum of the History of Ponce (Casa Salazar)**, 844-7071, open daily except Tuesdays from 9 A.M. to 5 P.M., admission $3 for adults and $1.50 for children; and the **Ponce Museum of Art**, 848-0505, open daily from 10

A.M. to 5 P.M., admission $4 for adults and $2 for children. Note that once you leave the center of town, there are very few street signs, so be sure to have a good map and a sense of humor.

Just south of town, past the Ponce Hilton at the end of Ruta 14 (Avenida Malecón), is La Guancha Paseo Tablado, a happening boardwalk on the water that is lined with bars, cafes, and restaurants. It's a hangout spot for both young and old *ponceños*. We like having a cold Medalla or piña colada and watching the crowd, boats (it's a marina, too), and water. The trade winds keep things cool too. There is also a pier where you can catch a boat to Caja de Muertos (Coffin Island). Rafi Bega (787-842-8546) runs a private company bringing people over to the island. You have to call to see what the current schedule is. On the island there is a gorgeous beach for swimming, an old lighthouse built in 1880, and excellent snorkeling.

Hotel Meliá, Calle Cristina 75, P.O. Box 1431, Ponce, PR 00733. Local: 787-842-0260, fax 787-841-3602.

Located adjacent to the Parque de Bombas, this family-owned and -operated hotel is very affordable and within walking distance of all the historic sites of central Ponce. There are 80 clean, simple (and somewhat retro-funky) but comfortable enough rooms, all with air conditioning, private bath, phone, and cable TV. Rooms on the high floors offer some nice views, especially those facing west and the Plaza Las Delicias. There is no pool, but there is a very pleasant garden terrace and a wonderful rooftop terrace where breakfast is served—it is also a great place for evening cocktails. There is a restaurant and bar at the hotel, and you are steps away from countless others. We loved the lobby's Spanish charm—tile floors, high ceilings, faded décor—and, the last time we visited, the counterpoint of plastic covers on the lampshades (so anti-chic!).

Rates are *Cheap* and up (EP).

Ponce Hilton & Casino, Avenida Caribe No. 1150, P.O. Box 7419, Ponce, PR 00731. Stateside and Canada: 800-HILTONS. Local: 787-259-7676, fax 787-259-7674.
Web site: www.hilton.com
e-mail: poncehil@coqui.com

Geared to the business traveler, the blue-and-white Ponce Hilton is the city's biggest hotel and the largest resort on Puerto Rico's south coast. Located about 10 minutes south of the Plaza Las Delicias (depending on traffic), we find this 153-room hotel lacking in warmth and charm. Indeed, the lobby has the feel of a suburban mall. The property has 80 acres, is on the waterfront (although the beach in front is not very pretty), and sea views are decent only from the top (fourth) floor. It does have a putting green and driving range, four lighted tennis courts, a pool, a fitness center, a basketball court, a playground, and a pool table (we love eight-ball). There are two restaurants, three bars (including the Pavilion Discotheque), and, of course, the casino. The rooms, furnished in rattan and tropical colors, are loaded with amenities, including air conditioning, lanai, cable TV with video games, speakerphone with voice mail and data port, safe, minibar, and iron and ironing board.

Rates are **Very Pricey** and up (EP). Look for packages or corporate discounts.

Guánica/La Parguera

Located on the southern coast of the island, west of Ponce and near three great natural sites—the Guánica Forest Reserve, the Phosphorescent Bay, and Gilligan's Island—Guánica is an example of the "real" Puerto Rico. There are few fast-food chains, 7-Elevens, or Blockbuster Videos—just lots of *bodegas* and *panaderías*. Guánica has a cool-looking waterfront (camera, please), and just outside of town, the Guánica Forest Reserve has some gorgeous and deserted beaches. To get to the Reserve, just follow Route 333 until you can go no farther. You'll see places to stop along the way. Guánica also has some of the best dive sites in Puerto Rico. Gilligan's Island is a small, uninhabited, mile-offshore cay with a secluded beach and excellent snorkeling. The folks at Copamarina, 821-0505, can arrange an excursion there.

About 10 miles west of Guánica is La Parguera and Phosphorescent Bay (Route 324—watch for signs). In the dark of a calm night, phosphorescent plankton (dinoflagellates, to be precise) create "sparks" when there's any movement in the water, as it disturbs their nesting. La Parguera's coastline is filled with mangrove islands and is not a beach destination. However, the harbor is a haven for fishing charters, especially the deep-sea variety. Call Parguera Fishing Charters (787-899-4698) for more info.

Copamarina Beach Resort, Route 333, Km 6.5, P.O. Box 805, Caña Gorda, Guánica, PR 00653-0805. Stateside: 800-468-4553. Local: 787-821-0505 or 800-981-4676, fax 787-821-0070. Web site: www.copamarina.com
e-mail: copamarina@coqui.net

Copamarina is a reasonably priced resort situated on the Bahía de Guánica in a quiet part of the island. It has recently expanded and now has 106 rooms and suites spread out over 16 acres. The rooms are attractive—with wall-to-wall carpeting or tiled floors, bamboo and light wood furnishings, air conditioning, cable TV, fridges, safes, hair dryers, coffeemakers, and phones—and they sport little lanais. The main lobby has a very pleasant veranda on which to sit and read.

This is a great place to go if you want to be somewhere tranquil and be near the extensive Guánica Forest Reserve (where you can take long walks or bike rides). Copamarina is very popular with weekenders from San Juan who want a secluded getaway. The grounds are well tended and the beach is pretty. The seas here are calm because the bay is sheltered. However, we don't like that the water at times can have lots of seaweed in it. There are nicer and seaweed-free beaches close by in the Forest Reserve. We also don't like the chain-link fence between the beach and the grounds (so unsightly). There are two pools, a kids' pool, full water sports—including a full-service PADI Dive Center—a small fitness center, and two lighted tennis courts. For dining, there is the open-air Las Palmas Café and Wilo's Coastal Cuisine. Wilo's offers both international and nouvelle Puerto Rican cuisine.

Rates are *Pricey* and up (EP).

Parador Villa Parguera, La Parguera, P.O. Box 273, Lajas, Puerto Rico 00667. Stateside: 800-443-0266. Local: 787-899-7777/3975, fax 787-899-6040. Web site: www.elshop.com
e-mail: elshop@elshop.com

RUM & REGGAE'S PUERTO RICO

An unassuming 70-room hotel on the water in La Parguera, Villa Parguera provides a comfortable yet simple place to stay while fishing or whatever in this area. It's popular on weekends with *sanjuaneros*, so advance reservations are a must. Rooms are standard motel fare, with air conditioning, cable TV, phone, private bath, and lanai. We suggest a room with a sea view. There is a small pool in which to refresh yourself and a breezy dock on which to enjoy a cocktail. A restaurant serving international and Puerto Rican fare and a bar and nightclub are on the premises.

Rates are **Cheap** (EP).

The West Coast
Boquerón

Located in an area called Cabo Rojo in the southwestern corner of the island, Boquerón used to be a charming little village but over the past decade it has grown tremendously. Boquerón has a beautiful, long beach and calm bay and is considered one of Puerto Rico's best bathing beaches. For this reason, it has become a very popular weekend getaway spot for *sanjuaneros* (just over a two-hour drive). The bay is very scenic, with mountains at the southern end. Actually, the entire area is quite wonderful. It's rural, with pastures and herds of cattle reaching up to green hills and mountains.

It's also a boat town—lots of cruising boats stop here, bringing with them those weathered and boozy "boat rats." Now, we're not one to bitch about a few cocktails. After all, Nick and Nora Charles (and, of course, Patsy Stone) are our idols. But these people start early, hang at the bar for hours, get totally blotto, and by a miracle of gravitation and balance, somehow manage to get back to their boats intact. They're always in their berths early because they get so trashed. We're amused as long as they don't start talking to us in an advanced state of inebriation. If they do, we excuse ourselves to go to the loo and never return.

The center of activity in Boquerón is the main intersection in town, by the bay, where there are two prominent bars on opposite corners. The one with the action and a very competitive pool table is called Shamar. You know it's a yachty favorite from all the tattered burgees and ensigns donated to the bar by boaters from yacht clubs and countries around the world.

Parador Boquemar, Route 101, P.O. Box 133, Boquerón, Cabo Rojo, PR 00622. Local: 787-851-2158, fax 787-851-7600.

This *parador* in Boquerón resembles a motel but is clean, efficient, and cheap. Recently renovated, this pink place has 75 rooms, all with air conditioning, fridge, phone, cable TV, and private bath. There is a swimming pool, a restaurant (La Cascada), and a bar. Rooms on the second and third floors have lanais. The town junction (where all the activity happens) and the beach are just around the corner and down the street. Be sure to make reservations well in advance, as the Boquemar is popular with folks from San Juan on weekends.

Rates are **Cheap** (EP).

Rincón

This corner of Puerto Rico is a surfer's mecca. Actually, some of the best surfing in the Caribbean is found here during the winter months. There are more than 20 surf spots in the Rincón-Aguadilla area, with names like "Dogman's," "Domes," and "Shithouse," and several surf shops. A visit to the local post office will turn up as many bleached-out surfer dudes as Puerto Ricans. Rincón is also one of the most Anglicized parts of the island. Some fun surfer hangouts are the **Calypso Tropical Café** (823-4151), in front of María's Beach by El Faro Park, and **Beside the Pointe** (823-8550), by Sandy Beach. For more info on Rincón, visit its Web site at http://home.coqui.net/seadog/rincon.htm. Pick up a copy of the tourist map for one dollar at many locations or visit the Tourist Information Center at 787-823-5024 at the intersection of Routes 413 and 115. A rental car is a must if you stay in the area. There is an airport in Aguadilla (about a 30-minute drive). Most people fly into San Juan (about 95 miles away and over a two-hour drive).

The Horned Dorset Primavera, Ruta 429, Km. 3.0, Apartado 1132, Rincón, PR 00677. Stateside and Canada: 800-633-1857. Local: 787-823-4030, fax 787-823-5580.

Web site: www.horneddorset.com

We love the Horned Dorset Primavera, a small and lovely four-acre property, tucked away on the coast south of Rincón (so tucked away we have driven by it on two separate occasions). It's a symphony of taste with a touch of attitude, and owners Harold Davies, Wilhelm Sack, and Kingsley Wratten have gone to great pains to make the property a tranquil and comfortable hideaway. They proudly claim that this is a place without activities—no pool aerobics, radios, TVs, or room phones (and cell phones are not allowed in the lobby!). Named after Davies and Wratten's first inn in upstate New York: it's well appointed, nicely decorated, has a very attractive staff and features a fantastic library. Readers will be thrilled. You can sink into a big comfy chair, order a drink, check out the spectacular western view of the water (or the staff), and occasionally look up to see who might be passing through the lobby—a piece of heaven to some, including us. Breakfast is served on the veranda of the main building or in your room (we had it on our lanai in our bathrobes—it is a great touch). Lunch is on the veranda or by the main pool. The hotel's prix fixe Dining Room, which we found a tad stuffy, features delicious French cuisine with Caribbean accents by chef Aaron Wratten. There is a small gym for the health-conscious and the hotel can arrange activities such as tennis, horseback riding, and diving.

There are 31 rooms and suites with four-poster mahogany beds and antiques, which make for very comfortable accommodation. There's even a separate eight-bedroom house called Casa Escondida for large groups. All rooms have lanais or terraces and all have ocean views, air conditioning and ceiling fans, and cushy sofas. The very large bathrooms have brass-claw-foot tubs, large vanities and mirrors (we love that—room for everyone's toiletries), and lots of white marble. The well-manicured grounds contain a medium-size pool, a smaller pool on the top of the hill by the Mesa Suites, private pools in five rooms, and a tiny beach for sunning and swimming. But we'd say the main reason to come here is to read, be quiet, spend time with your companion, and enjoy great food or maybe have that secret tryst with that certain someone. The hotel does not have facilities for children and no one under 12 is accepted as a guest. We say hooray for the HDP! No crying babies, strollers, or whining kids to distract us from the latest Danielle Steele.

The hotel's acknowledged success (Zagat awarded it its highest-rated hotel and restaurant in the Caribbean in 2001), has apparently convinced the owners to expand their enterprise. Construction of 22 one-bedroom villas on property adjoining the hotel has begun. We're told they will be offered for sale as condominiums and the hotel will offer rental management services. Each villa will have its own individual pool. There will also be a larger pool and Jacuzzi. We hope the new addition won't spoil the secluded ambiance of the Horned Dorset. We're also told a new fitness center is on the way. It will be a welcome addition.

Rates are *Ridiculous* (EP). Add $160 per couple per day for MAP (recommended).

Lemontree Waterfront Cottages, Ruta 429, Box 200, Rincón, PR 00677. Local: 787-823-6452, fax 787-823-5821.
Web site: www.lemontreepr.com
e-mail: info@lemontreepr.com

Just down the road from the ultra-fancy Horned Dorset is this sort of funky place. Located so close to the water that a misstep will virtually put you in the drink, the Lemontree is two houses linked together by a patio. The property has a seawall, steps down to the water, and a sliver of sand (and we mean sliver). Owned and operated by Lov and Lora Carabello, there are a total of six efficiency units—two studios, two one-bedroom "cottages," one two-bedroom and one three-bedroom apartment. All have lanais facing west and the Mona Passage (we love the views), and all come with fully equipped kitchens (with blender, coffeemaker, and microwave), tile floors, cable TV, air conditioning in the bedrooms, some custom woodwork, and simple rattan furnishings. The three-bedroom Papaya unit has a wet bar on the lanai. Maid service and linen change occurs halfway through your stay. Laundry service is available for a small fee.

Rates are *Not So Cheap* and up (EP). There is a three-night minimum.

Villa Cofresí, Ruta 115, Km 12.0, P.O. Box 874, Rincón, PR 00677. Local: 787-823-2450, fax 787-823-1770.
Web site: www.villacofresi.com
e-mail: info@villacofresi.com

Villa Cofresí sits right on a great swimming beach. Motelish in look with no visual or ambient appeal, there are 63 clean and simple rooms, all with air conditioning, cable TV, and fridges. The large rooms have tiled floors and drop ceilings, all-tile baths with new fixtures. All of the recently added rooms face the ocean. A restaurant, bar, pool, and kayaking round out the facilities. Don't expect a groovy crowd here, but it's reasonably priced. Anti-chic seekers may like this place. The hotel's restaurant serves seafood, steaks and traditional Puerto Rican cuisine from 5–10 P.M.

Rates are *Not So Cheap* (EP).

Parador Villa Antonio, Ruta 115, Km 12.3, P.O. Box 68, Rincón, PR 00677. Stateside and Canada: 800-443-0266. Local: 787-823-2645, fax 787-823-3380.
Web site: www.villa-antonio.com
e-mail: pva@villa-antonio.com

One of the *paradores de Puerto Rico,* Villa Antonio is next door to Villa Cofresí and what it lacks in ambience—it's low, squat pink buildings aren't very visually appealing—it makes up with a wonderful swimming beach. There are 61 air-conditioned units with kitchenettes. Rooms are basic motel fare and have phones, cable TV, daily maid service, and lanais. There is are two pools, a children's play area, a game room, and two tennis courts. A good budget choice for families.

Rates are *Cheap* and up (EP).

Where to Eat

The West Coast: Boquerón

There are several restaurants in town, including **Parador Boquemar,** 851-2158, serving a Continental seafood menu ($$$). Just up the coast, Joyuda is known for its seafood and has several good restaurants, including **El Bohío,** 851-2755, Carretera 102, Km 13.9, Caribbean/seafood menu ($$$); **Perichi's,** 851-3131, Carretera 102, Km 14.3, international/seafood menu ($$$); and **Tino's,** 851-2976, Carretera 102, Km 13.5, seafood menu ($$$). In the morning, there are several little breakfast spots next to the happening bars, which are cheap and simple.

Rincón

Besides the **Horned Dorset** ($$$$$), try the **Lazy Parrot**, 823-5654, located one mile from El Faro on Carretera No. 413, Km 4.1, Bo. Puntas, Rincón, serving a mixed menu—including vegetarian ($$$). Virtually next door to the Horned Dorset, **El Molino del Quijote**, 823-4010, Ruta 429, Km 3.3, is open Friday through Sunday and serves Puerto Rican/Spanish cuisine ($$$). For a real Puerto Rican dining experience, check out **Las Colinas,** 868-8686, at Parador J.B. Hidden Village, Ruta 4416, Km. 2.5, Sector Villa Rubia in neighboring Aguada. Every day until 11. ($$$).

North Coast
Dorado

Two sister resorts, built by the Rockefellers' RockResorts company in 1958 (Dorado Beach) and 1972 (Cerromar Beach) and purchased by Hyatt in 1985, share a 1,000-acre former grapefruit and coconut plantation just west of the town of Dorado and 22 miles west of San Juan. This is Puerto Rico's premier resort, with more than two miles of beaches and coastline, four 18-hole Championship golf courses (some of the best in the Caribbean), 14 hardclay tennis courts (two lighted), a windsurfing and water sports center, the River Pool, an 82-foot lap pool, two Olympic-size pools and two kid's pools, eight restaurants, cafés, and snack bars, two casinos, and more than 800 guest rooms. The grounds are beautifully planted and well maintained, as you would expect the Rockefellers would have wanted it. Indeed, this is one of the lushest, most attractively landscaped properties in the tropics. Su Casa (Dorado Beach), a seasonal restaurant that serves Spanish and Puerto Rican cuisine, is in the original plantation house.

The two resorts share the same huge property but are distinctly different in character. Dorado Beach, the older of the two, has the classic RockResorts look—low-key two-story buildings, breezy and tastefully designed lobbies and common areas with subtly stated elegance in the décor and furnishings. The total concept is to provide quiet luxury while fully integrating the natural setting with the design. A first-time visitor would have no idea how big the resort is by driving up to the main building. Everything is spread out and landscaped to make you feel as though you're staying at a small country club. And the repeat clientele who stay here prefer it that way and don't like any change. Dorado looks much the way it did 40 years ago. On the other hand, Cerromar impresses you as a big, splashy resort where lots is happening all the time. The design is totally different from Dorado Beach. This is a seven-story hotel with several wings and pavilions. With all the activity, Cerromar is preferred by families or those who need lots going on. Guests of both resorts have reciprocal privileges, so Cerromar guests can golf, dine, or beach at Dorado and Dorado guests can hang out at Cerromar at will—a nice feature.

Dorado Beach and Cerromar Beach are a golfer's paradise. There are four 18-hole Robert Trent Jones II Championship courses (called North, South, East, and West) on flat and rolling terrain that will challenge all golfers. They have been the site of numerous golf tournaments. All feature Mr. Jones's trademarks: huge greens, lots of bunkers and water hazards, and long fairways. Probably the toughest links are the East and West courses. The East, at 6,985 yards, has the super-tough 13th hole, a double-dog-leg, 540-yard, two-pond nightmare. The West, at 6,913 yards, has the toughest par-3s at the resort, spiting you with sloping greens and mucho bunkers. The North course is a 6,841-yard links-style course, and the South, at 7,047 yards, is a challenge of winds and mega water hazards. Greens fees are $70 to $100 for guests and $100 to $145 for nonguests. Carts are $20 per person (mandatory) and club rentals are $40. Golf packages are available.

Hyatt Dorado Beach Resort and Country Club, Highway 693, Dorado, PR 00646. Stateside and Canada: 800-233-1234. Local: 787-796-1234, fax 787-796-2022.
Web site: www.hyatt.com

Pulling up to the entrance of the hotel, past a fleet of golf carts parked by guests, you walk into a very elegant and comfortable lobby with tile floors, objets d'art, and an advantageously angled location for generous ocean views and trade wind breezes. There are beaches on both sides of the main building—a man-made reef keeps the lagoon water fairly calm from the turbulent Atlantic and makes it great for swimming. There are two restaurants, the rather

RUM & REGGAE'S PUERTO RICO

dressy Surf Room (jackets required) and the screened-in Ocean Terrace (to keep out the birds who like to help guests eat their meals), and a small casino that is open only in the winter (guests use Cerromar's in the off-season). A third restaurant, the intimate and exclusive Su Casa, is located down the beach in the old plantation house and is also seasonal. We love the full-service Le Spa Health & Beauty Center, for pampering and pecs.

The 262 guest rooms fan out in both directions from the main building. The best, of course, are the beachfront units. They come in two versions—upstairs and downstairs. The downstairs units have two double beds (better for families or nonintimate roommates), whereas the upstairs units have one king-size bed. The floors are tiled with terra-cotta and the furnishings are comfortable and tropical. Given that this place was built in the '50s, it still holds its own quite well (there have been many updates). The *casitas* (suites), of which there are 17, are about the same size and much more expensive. They are exemplary in the spacious and naturally lit bathrooms (the shower roof is a greenhouse). A patio in front leads to the beach. For the money, however, you're better off at the beachfront units (and the terraces are more private). All rooms are air conditioned and have voice mail, cable TV, video messages-account review, check-out, room safes (and safe deposit boxes at the front desk for your jewels), minibars, irons and ironing boards, and bathrobes. We love the 24-hour room service for those late-night Cosmopolitans.

Rates are **Beyond Belief** (EP). Look for packages and corporate discounts.

Hyatt Regency Cerromar Beach Resort & Casino, Highway 693, Dorado, PR 00646. Stateside and Canada: 800-233-1234. Local: 787-796-1234, fax 787-796-4647.
Web site: www.hyatt.com

Cerromar Beach is a multiwinged seven-story building with 506 guest rooms and a big-resort feel (the lobby looks much like an airline terminal). It is very popular with conventions because the facilities are bigger and geared to handle more than the Dorado's (there's also a Business Center here). Families also love it, with its huge River Pool complex, a bigger and wider beach than Dorado, and activities geared for adults and kids of all ages. Where Dorado is very quiet, Cerromar is bustling with activity— especially the casino in the evening. One of Cerromar's unique features is the River Pool—at 1,776 feet long, it's the longest current-propelled pool in the world. It moves water at 22,600 gallons per minute, and has 14 waterfalls and four water slides. The slide at its conclusion is three stories high and requires stairs to climb, but it is a blast. Be prepared to get a noseful of water from the splashdown (we did). While the whole River Pool idea is contrived (it was added in the '80s to attract families and vacationers who like the mega-resorts), it is different, fun, and both adults and kids will enjoy it (there is a bar with barstools in the water about halfway down, for a quick piña colada). Another great program for kids and teens (and for their parents because it gets the kids out of their hair) is Camp Hyatt. This service is for ages 3 to 15 and provides supervised activities from 9 A.M. to 4 P.M., and again from 6 to 10 P.M. (now *that*'s a vacation!). The cost is $40 per day per child and well worth it (you receive a 50 percent discount on the second room rental if the kids are enrolled). There are four restaurants (including Swan Cafe and Medici's), four bars, and a casino on the property.

The rooms at Cerromar are very comfortable and attractively furnished, with marble baths. All rooms have air conditioning, voice mail, cable TV, video messages-account review, check-out, room safes (and safe deposit boxes at the front desk), mini-bars, irons, and ironing boards. Some rooms have data ports, and the Regency Club guests get bathrobes (only during high season but we're not sure why—maybe low-season guests get teddies?). As with Dorado Beach, we love the 24-hour room service for those late-night shots of tequila (variety is the spice of life).

Rates are **Ridiculous** and up (EP). Look for packages or corporate discounts.

Don't Miss

El Yunque—You can't visit Puerto Rico without a visit to El Yunque (officially the Caribbean National Forest and part of the U.S. National Forest system). It is a great example of a rain forest for those who have never seen one before, although it was ravaged by 1998's Hurricane Georges. Evidence of the deadly storm is apparent everywhere, but this being the tropics, recovery is remarkably quick.

El Yunque is only about an hour's drive east of San Juan and it is almost impossible to drive to the summit (which was possible before Hurricanes Hugo and Georges). The drive up to the Visitors Center takes you past towering banks of green ferns and canopies of trees and vines. The Forest itself consists of 28,000 acres and is the largest and wettest in the U.S. National Forest system (240 inches, or 100 billion gallons, of water fall on the forest every year). Note that there are no poisonous snakes on Puerto Rico. Be sure to stop at the Sierra Palma, an interpretive center located at Km. 11.6 on Route 91, just before the parking area, for information on the hiking trails; open daily from 9:30 A.M. to 5 P.M., except on Christmas Day (787-888-1880).

If you decide to hike (you should), the first section of the trail to the summit of El Yunque is a well-worn concrete path. While a steady climb, it is fairly easy but very humid (remember—rain forest). The second section turns into a path which, while a little muddy, is rather easy to walk. If you walk at a steady pace, you can make it to the summit in one hour (we did). For the length of the trail, you will be walking through forest. Some people may be over the whole concept in 15 minutes and will turn around. The few vista points you come to, including the towers, are more often than not shrouded in clouds, so don't expect spectacular vistas; expect the forest and its hundreds of varieties of foliage and birds (which you hear more often than see). In this age of sound bites and short attention spans, if you don't like the forest you will be bored fairly quickly. Once you get near the top, there is a choice—you'll reach a fork in the road. We recommend going to the tower, which is a scant .3 kilometer away. The temptation is to go to the peak of El Yunque, because it *is* the summit. However, when you get to the peak, there are at least seven huge microwave transmission towers to thoroughly irradiate you (or at least there were before Hurricane Georges). And since the clouds usually block the view, these lovely structures will be what you see. The only advantage to going to the peak is that you can take the road down (open to official vehicles only) —which is a faster route.

Scenic Drives—There are several on this very scenic island. The two we would recommend are a half-day and an overnight journey from San Juan, respectively.

Trip One takes you east on Route 3 to Luquillo, the location of a great local beach (the drive between San Juan and Luquillo is pretty hideous), and south past Fajardo and the very pretty Playa de Naguabo. It continues on Route 3 past industrial Humacao and into sugarcane territory. When you get to Yabucoa, you start to climb through some very winding mountain roads with great vistas of the valley and the sea (watch out for the cane trucks—don't worry, you'll hear their horns). The road descends to Maunabo and eventually follows the sea along the Caribbean. When you get to Guayama, take Route 15 north to Cayey. This is incredibly scenic—lots of mountain vistas and lush foliage and vegetation. At Cayey, hook on to the highway (Route 52) and head north back to San Juan.

Trip Two takes you through the Cordillera Central, the mountainous spine of Puerto Rico. This is a long, twist-and-turn drive, so leave early in the morning for a relaxing pace. Arrange to stay in Boquerón or Rincón at the other end of the road. Take Route 52 south from San Juan, get off in Cayey, and take Route 14 to Coamo and the Baños de Coamo (hot springs), where you can enjoy a natural hot tub. From Coamo, take Route 150 west past Lago Tao Vaga, through the tiny town of Villaba. At Villaba, head north on Route 149 until you reach the junction of Route 143. Turn left (west) and enjoy this stretch of majestic scenery. This road will take you past the biggest mountains in Puerto Rico, including Cerro de Punta, Puerto Rico's highest peak at 4,390 feet. At the junction of Route 10 (not the highway under construction but the secondary road just beyond), head north until you get to Route 518. If you've had enough and you have enough daylight left to head back to San Juan (you'll need at least three hours), continue on Route 10 (it will eventually meet the completed part of Highway 10, which you should take) until you reach the junction of Route 22, then go east on 22. If you want to continue, take Route 518 to Route 525. About five kilometers later is the junction of Route 135. Turn left (west) on Route 135 until the junction of Route 128. Turn left again (south) on Route

128 and follow to Route 365. Take Route 365, which will merge into Route 366. At the junction of Route 120, turn right (north) on Route 120 and continue until Route 106. Turn left (west) on Route 106 and follow this all the way to Mayagüez. Once in Mayagüez, Route 2 north takes you to the Rincón area and Route 2 south to Route 100 to Boquerón.

Río Camuy Cave Park—Everyone raves about these "oh you've got to see them," caves. Personally, the last thing we want to do in the tropics is go subterranean. However, they *are* a wonder and kids will love them. Located near Lares, tours are conducted via trolley. Open Wednesday from 8 A.M. to 4 P.M. You must call ahead to reserve a space on the tour (787-898-3100 or 787-763-0568).

Arecibo Observatory—Home of the world's largest radio telescope (the radar dish is over 1,000 feet in diameter, 565 feet deep, and covers 20 acres), the Observatory and its scientists listen for signs of life in the universe. It is part of the National Astronomy and Ionosphere Center and is operated by Cornell University in conjunction with the National Science Foundation. Viewers of several movies, including *Contact* and an early 007 movie we can't remember the name of, will recognize the dish. A new visitors center provides exhibits and a great view of the Observatory. Open Wednesday through Friday from 12 to 4 P.M., weekends and holidays from 9 A.M. to 4 P.M. Admission is $4 for adults and $2 for kids and seniors. Call 787-878-2612 for more information.

Nature Resorts—While we have not been here, the buzz is interesting enough about this place that we will mention it. In a jungle-like mountain setting in Utuado (near the Camuy Caves) is **Hotel La Casa Grande** (888-343-2272 or 787-894-3939/3900, www.hotelcasagrande.com). Once the hacienda for a 5,000-acre ranch, the old house and surroundings have been turned into a 20-room inn and restaurant by ex–New Yorkers Steven and Marlene Weingarten.

Windsurfing and Surfing in Rincón—If you're a windsurfer or surfer, this is one of the best places to do both in the Caribbean. Many championships in both sports are held at Surfer and Wilderness Beaches, and there is a growing California-style surfer community.

Guánica—A wonderful and scenic town for those in search of the real Puerto Rico (see Guánica section).

Fitness City —If you need a gym to keep those *pecs* and *bis* in shape for the beach and going out while in San Juan, this gym in Ocean Park offers reasonable daily and weekly passes and an English-speaking staff. Call Fitness City at 268-7773 (1959 Loiza, top floor).

Lunch at Hostería del Mar and Dinner at Pamela's—Our favorite spots for lunch and dinner in San Juan are in Ocean Park (see "Where to Eat").

Culebra and Vieques—These two small islands off the east coast of Puerto Rico offer a fun day-trip, overnight excursion, or entire holiday. See the Culebra and Vieques chapters.

Que Pasa?—Published by the Puerto Rico Tourism Company, this is an great free publication to peruse for events and the latest info. It also has an ample listing of hotels and restaurants in Puerto Rico. For a free copy, call 800-223-6530 from the U.S. or 721-2400 in Puerto Rico, or visit their Web site: www.prtourism.com.

Museo de Arte de Puerto Rico—Opened in 2000, the new museum incorporates part of the old San Juan Municipal Hospital designed in the neo-classical style by William Shimmelphening with a brand new modern architectural five-story gem designed by Otto Reyes and Luis Guiterrez. The museum has more than 130,000 square feet of exhibition space and a three-story atrium called the Great Hall. Puerto Rican art throughout the island's history is on display here. Finally, Puerto Rico has a world-class art exhibition space! Located on Ave. de Diego 299 in Santurce, it's open Tuesday through Saturday from 10 A.M. to 5 P.M. (Wednesdays until 8 P.M.), Sundays from 11 A.M. to 6 P.M. Admission is $5 for adults and $3 for kids and seniors. Call 787-977-6277 or go to www.mapr.org for more info.

CULEBRA

Touristo Scale: 👤 👤 👤 (3)

Overview

WE HAD JUST MISSED the last flight from Fajardo to Culebra. A split-second decision to charter a plane, and off we went on a six-seater Britten Islander. It was a dramatic exit. But that was nothing compared to what greeted us upon our arrival. Our "limo" was a beat-up old VW van, with no door and two plastic deck chairs for seats. Our hostess was an American woman with 12 children who lived in a trailer where goats came and went and had eaten most of the upholstery. Welcome to Culebra—the land of the *very* laid-back. Culebra is a small and simple island. Politically part of the Commonwealth of Puerto Rico, it is light-years away from the fast pace of San Juan. Although Spanish is the primary language here, English is spoken everywhere. The main village on the island is Dewey, named for Admiral George Dewey, an American hero of the Spanish-American War. This is where the ferry docks, the post office, and most of the commerce are located. There are only a few hundred hotel rooms on the island, a few good restaurants, and no nightclubs, discos, or casinos. The pace is slow, slow, slow! Overall, one gets the impression that this is what the Caribbean used to be like. Indeed, *culebrenses*—as residents are called—are very covetous of their way of life and are very suspect of any change, or "progress." Their attitude is one of "leave us alone." So far, they've been successful. Actually, Hurricanes Hugo (1989), Luís (1995), and Georges (1998) have helped their cause tremendously by hurting the flourishing tourist trade in both damaged accommodations and bad publicity.

Culebra is not a lush, verdant island. Rather, it's very dry and arid. But its star attraction, besides its unspoiledness, is its beaches—some of the most beautiful in the Caribbean. Two of our Top Ten Puerto Rico Beaches are here, Flamenco and Soni. Even on a busy day, there is always lots of space on this huge stretch of blindingly white sand.

Culebra is not for everyone. It's rustic, and if you expect to be pampered or entertained, forget it, it's not for you. But if you don't mind simple accommodations, cooking for yourself a lot or eating at mostly simple restaurants, and tons of quiet, then you'll love it. Probably the best analogy is that of a Cinderella who *didn't* want to go the ball. She purposely stays out of the spotlight cast on her star stepsisters, Puerto Rico and St. Thomas, loving the solitude. She is one of the Caribbean's best-kept secrets—an island where the pace is that of yesteryear, the beaches are gorgeous, and attitude nonexistent.

The Briefest of Histories (Really!)

Culebra was not inhabited by Europeans until the very late date of 1886, when it was settled by the Spanish (it was part of the Spanish Virgin Islands). It was ceded to the U.S. as part of the settlement of the Spanish-American War. The U.S. incorporated it into the Commonwealth of Puerto Rico, where it has remained ever since. In 1909 President Theodore Roosevelt designated the former Spanish Crown lands (2,800 acres) a National Wildlife Refuge, to protect the native seabird colonies (although the U.S. Navy used it for bombing practice from World War II until 1975). Today this area is administered by the U.S. Fish and Wildlife Service.

Culebra: Key Facts

LOCATION	18°N by 65°W
	17 miles east of Fajardo, Puerto Rico
	12 miles west of St. Thomas
	1,660 miles southeast of New York
SIZE	7 miles long by 3 miles wide
HIGHEST POINT	Mt. Resaca (650 ft.)
POPULATION	About 1,868

LANGUAGE	Spanish, English
TIME	Atlantic Standard Time (1 hour ahead of EST, same as EDT)
AREA CODE	787 (must be dialed with all calls locally)
ELECTRICITY	110 volts AC, 60 cycles
CURRENCY	The U.S. dollar
DRIVING	On the *right*; valid driver's license okay
DOCUMENTS	U.S. citizens do not have to have a passport or visa. Canadians should have a passport or proof of citizenship with ID; U.K. visitors need a passport and visa
DEPARTURE TAX	None
BEER TO DRINK	Medalla
RUM TO DRINK	Don Q or Bacardi
MUSIC TO HEAR	Salsa!
TOURISM INFO	800-223-6530 www.culebra-island.com www.culebra.org

Getting There

San Juan is the primary gateway to the Caribbean and is reached by most major U.S. carriers. From San Juan and Fajardo, **Vieques Air Link** (787-722-3736 in Isla Verde/San Juan, 787-742-0254 in Culebra, or 787-863-3020 in Fajardo) has regularly scheduled service. **Isla Nena** (877-812-5144 or 787-742-0972) also has scheduled service from San Juan's Luis Muñoz Marín International Airport. They also occasionally fly from Vieques if there is demand. For those who don't want to fly, there is passenger and car ferry service from Fajardo daily; call the Fajardo Port Authority at 787-742-3161 or 787-863-0705 for the current schedules.

Getting Around

While there is good minivan taxi service (*públicos*) between Dewey and Playa Flamenco, a jeep or car is a good idea for getting to other beaches, the grocery store, and just general mobility. There are several people and outfits who rent cars, including **Prestige Car Rental** (787-742-3242), **Jerry's Jeeps** (787-742-0587), **R & W Jeep Rental** (787-742-0563), **Carlos Jeep Rental** (787-742-3514), **Coral Reef Car Rental** (787-742-0055), **Dick & Cathy** (787-742-0062), **Jr. Acosta** (787-742-3518), and **Tamarindo Car Rental** (787-742-0050). There is a full-service bike shop in Dewey called **Culebra Bikes Shop** (787-742-2209), which rents mountain bikes. **Dick & Cathy** (787-742-0062) also rent bikes.

Focus on Culebra: The Beaches

For such a small island, there are some amazing beaches here. The lack of development has saved most of them from the usual Caribbean resort blight. Two of the beaches, Resaca and Brava, are nesting sites for leatherback turtles and are off-limits from April 1 to August 30. They are also hard to get to (the best way is by boat). Since shade is minimal at all Culebra beaches, *be sure to bring a beach umbrella* so you don't get burned to a crisp.

We vacillate between which is the best beach on the island, Soni or Flamenco. In a previous edition of *Rum & Reggae's Caribbean,* we decided it was Soni (also spelled Zoni), at the eastern end of the island, with its wide stretch of white sand, calm surf, and no people. There are great views of the islets of Culebrita and Cayo Norte across the bay, and far in the distance St. Thomas. To get there, take the eastern road as far as it will go. You will see cars parked where the road gets really bad. Park there, and walk the remaining 100 yards down to the beach. There are no facilities and no shade at the beach, so be sure to bring water and an umbrella.

This time, we're mad for Flamenco, Culebra's most popular strand and now our favorite, too. Flamenco is one of our Top Ten Caribbean Beaches. A mile-long arc of totally white, powdery sand set in a large cove, this is truly a beautiful beach. Its exposure to the northern Atlantic allows for good bodysurfing, especially in the winter months. It can get busy on summer weekends and during Puerto Rican holidays. At the parking area there are rest rooms and picnic tables. If you walk to the left, you'll come to a very secluded part of the beach, especially if you go around the rocky coral point.

In the past, people have camped out for free (and illegally) for long periods of time in the Hurricane Hugo–destroyed remnants of an old army post here. But this practice does not seem to be tolerated as much today. On the western end of the beach is Culebra Beach Villas & Resort, a camp lodge–like place with a beach bar that's popular with Puerto Rican families. To get to Flamenco, take the road that passes the airport (the runway will be on your right), and follow it to the end.

Other beaches to explore on the island are Tamarindo (rocky), Impact (great snorkeling), and Tortuga (very private). There is also a wonderful little beach on the islet of Luis Peña and two gorgeous beaches on Culebrita. The latter can easily be reached by hiring a boat: *Muff the Magic Fun Boat*—talk to Jack or Pat (787-397-7497).

Where to Stay

Ah, there's the rub! Culebra, in our opinion, needs a groovy little place like the Inn on the Blue Horizon or Hacienda Tamarindo on its sister Vieques. There just aren't many good options here. In Dewey, there are three guest houses we like: Villa Boheme, Posada La Hamaca, and Mamacita's. There are also several condos or villa properties, which may be the best way to go because then you'll have a kitchen.

Villa Boheme, 368 Fulladoza Street, Culebra, PR 00775. Local: 787-742-3508, fax same.
Web site: www.villahomeme.com
e-mail: villaboheme@juno.com
    Set in a nice, breezy location right on Ensenada Bay, this would be our first choice for lodging on Culebra. It's also within easy walking distance of town and restaurants. A symphony of beige and mauve, all rooms are simple and comfortable and feature air conditioning, ceiling fans, and private baths. A communal kitchen is available for guests. There are also efficiency apartments with fully equipped kitchens and private lanais. The Villa has a large lanai with chaises and chairs, a great place for a cocktail.
    Rates are *Cheap* and up (EP).

Posada La Hamaca, Calle Castelar No. 68, P.O. Box 388, Dewey, Culebra, PR 00775. Local: 787-742-3516, fax 787-742-0181. Web site: www.posada.com

Located right in Dewey on the canal by the drawbridge, Posada La Hamaca was one of the original guest houses on the island. This wonderfully clean and comfortable place is still a good choice for in-town accommodation. Situated in a simple Spanish-style house, there are six double rooms and three efficiency units (i.e., with kitchenettes or kitchens). Each room has a private bath, air conditioning, and ceiling fan. The Posada provides free ice, coolers, and towels for the beach. But the best thing about Posada La Hamaca is the managers, Pat and Jack, who are very friendly and helpful and seem to know more about the island than anyone.

Rates are *Cheap* (EP).

Mamacita's Guest House, Calle Castelar, Box 818, Dewey, Culebra, PR 00775. Local: 787-742-0090.

This is a small, brightly colored guest house located right next door to Posada La Hamaca. Mamacita's also has a pretty and colorful patio on the canal, serving breakfast, lunch, and dinner. There are only six rooms, located above the restaurant in decked spaces. The room on the top floor has the best views, including a sweeping vista of the harbor. All rooms have air conditioning, private baths, lanais, and ceiling fans.

Rates are *Cheap* (EP).

Villa Fulladoza, P.O. Box 162, Culebra, PR 00775. Local: 787-742-3576.

Situated right on the water with nice views of Ensenada Honda, this is a popular, interesting, and somewhat eclectically decorated ("homemade" was the word they used to describe the décor) complex within a 10-minute walk of town. Each of the seven units has a fully equipped kitchenette, ceiling and/or floor fans, and private bath. There is a boat dock and moorings available to those who have boats.

Rates are *Cheap* (EP).

Bayview Villas, Culebra, PR 00775-0775. Local: 787-742-3392 or 787-783-2961.

Situated on a hill overlooking Ensenada Honda and within walking distance of town, these are good villa accommodations on the island. There are three units (one has two bedrooms and two baths, one has two bedrooms and one and a half baths, and the other has one bedroom and one bath). Both are multileveled, with lots of Brazilian hardwood, sloped ceilings, large windows, tiled floors, and air conditioning. The fully equipped kitchens have a dishwasher, a gas grill, and a washing machine. The baths are spacious and tiled, and ceiling fans keep the breeze moving should the trade winds die down. Each unit has a large deck with hammocks and chaises.

Rates are *Pricey* and up. (EP). Weekly rentals only.

Harbour View Villas, P.O. Box 216, Culebra, PR 00775. Stateside: 800-440-0070. Local: 787-742-3855, fax 787-742-3171.
Web site: www.harbourviewvillas.com
e-mail: druso@culebrahotel.com

These rather space age–looking villas on stilts sit just outside of Dewey on the road to Melones Beach. Large lanais, lots of wood, 12-foot-high ceilings, big windows, and French doors with views of Bahia de Sardinas are the main features. The two villas, a one-bedroom and a two-bedroom, come with fully equipped kitchens, ceiling fans, and a living room. There are also three suites with kitchens, tiled baths, and air-conditioned bedrooms at the top of the five-acre property. You'll want to have a four-wheel-drive vehicle or a lot of nerve to negotiate the steep and treacherous driveway. We find these rustic accomodations a lot like a Vermont cabin—with mosquito netting over the beds for pioneer-like protection against the bugs. For any event, the harbor views are spectacular!

Rates are *Not So Cheap* and up (EP).

Culebra Beach Villas, Playa Flamenco, Culebra, PR 00775. Local: 787-754-6236.
Web site: www.culebrabeachrental.com
e-mail: jimmy@culebrabeachrental.com

The best thing about Culebra Beach Villas is the location—right on Playa Flamenco. It looks somewhat like a ski lodge with satellites cabins and is popular with Puerto Rican families. Don't expect much, as "rustic" is the buzzword here. But the management is friendly and there's that gorgeous beach in front. The 33 units (18 in concrete villas, 15 in a multi-story hotel) come with basic amenities like a fridge, microwave, stove, air conditioning, barbecue, TV, and private bath.

Rates are *Not So Cheap* and up (EP).

Hostal Bahía Marina, P.O. Box 188, Culebra, P.R. 00775. Local: 787-742-0366, 787-403-3079, or 787-501-0418, fax 787-742-0366. Web site: www. culbera-island.com
email: hostal@prtc.net

Located less than a mile away from the Bayview Villas, this newer property makes up with views what it lacks in architectural appearance. Several plain-looking buildings with three-room suites and standard rooms are perched high on a hill overlooking the Ensenada Honda. The driveway is steep and had us gripping the wheel in fright. Up top, you're rewarded with a pool and ratan-furnished rooms, all with air conditioning and satellite TV. There's not much ambience—or landscaping—to speak of, but the views are excellent.

Rates are *Not So Cheap* and up.

Where to Eat

There aren't many choices, and don't expect *haute cuisine*. Here's what we recommend:

Club Seabourne, 742-3169. Just past Bayview Villas overlooking the Ensenada Honda. A great place for dinner. Open only on weekends. $$

Dinghy Dock, on the road to Ensenada Honda in Dewey, 742-0233. Culebra's most popular restaurant for breakfast and dinner sits on the water and features grilled local seafood (lobster, grouper, yellowtail, and tuna). They also serve lunch. Open 7:30 A.M. to 10 P.M. $$$

El Batey, on the airport road by the baseball field, 742-3828. *Culebrensas* rave about El Batey's sandwiches. Open from 8 A.M. to 2 P.M. $

El Caobo (Tina's), Barriada Clark, 742-3235. In the neighborhood between Dewey and the airport, this small, funky place serves good, cheap Puerto Rican cuisine. Open daily. $

Mamacita's, Calle Castelar, Dewey, 742-0090. This colorful and pleasant patio by the canal is the setting for affordable lunch and dinner (and Ben & Jerry's ice cream). It's also a great place for a cocktail. Open 10:30 A.M. to 4 P.M. for lunch ($$) and 6 to 9 P.M. for dinner. Reservations suggested on weekends. $$$

Don't Miss

Paradise Gift Shop—A great place for groovy souvies, this shop, located right next to Mamacita's on Calle Castelar in Dewey (742-3569), is a must stop. Open daily from 9 A.M. to 2 P.M. and 5 to 8 P.M.

Isla de Culebra Tourist Guide—For $2.50, this is a good thing to buy when you arrive. Available at most shops including Paradise.

La Loma Gift Shop—Owned by Bruce and Kathie Goble, creators of the Culebra Island website, www.culebra-island.com. Located in downtown Dewey steps from the bridge leading to the fire station. Bruce and Kathie are a wealth of information on the island. You can also pick up a copy of the Isla Culebra Tourist Guide at their store.

The Culebra Calendar—This local monthly newspaper is a good source of Culebra happenings during your visit.

Water Sports—With all these beautiful beaches (and no streams or rivers to cloud the water), get thee out on them! For diving (depths range up to 100 feet and the reefs are in great shape), call the **Culebra Dive Shop** (cell: 787-507-4656), **Culebra Divers** (787-742-0803), or **Spa Ventures** (787-742-0581). You can rent kayaks at villa Boheme.

VIEQUES

ATLANTIC OCEAN

PUNTA ESTE

CAMP GARCIA
U.S. MARINE CORPS

BLUE BEACH

RED BEACH

GARCIA BEACH

BARRACUDA BAY
(BIOLUMINESCENT)

MOSQUITO BAY
(BIOLUMINESCENT)

MEDIA LUNA

CARIBBEAN SEA

ISABEL II

MARTINEAU BAY RESORT

CASA CIELO

MOSQUITO PEIR

CROW'S NEST

LA FINCA CARIBE

PILÓN

CASA DEL FRANCES

997

SUN BAY

BANANA GUEST HOUSE

TRADE WINDS

ESPERANZA

HACIENDA TAMARINDO

INN ON THE BLUE HORIZON

MONTE PIRATA (993 FT.)

U.S. NAVAL RESERVATION

GREEN BEACH

201

200

996

995

VIEQUES

Touristo Scale: 👤 👤 👤 👤 (4)

Overview

ONE OF OUR FIRST IMPRESSIONS upon arriving in Vieques was the abundance of wild horses meandering along the roads, seemingly without a care in the world. This caused us to ponder, not only about what were all those horses doing on the roads, but why were they so carefree? We later discovered why the horses are here—Spaniards left them behind centuries ago. With an abundance of territory to roam in due to the huge U.S. military base here and former navy lands now set aside for conservation, they have proliferated, and the locals don't seem to care about them. But what about the horse's Holly Golightly attitude? Our cat Jada has made us very attuned to the mood swings of animals, so we surmised that the horses feel just the weight of humans—not the weight of the world—on their shoulders. Karmically, we began to feel more relaxed and mellow for no apparent reason *at that very moment*. It was as if a Marin County zeitgeist had suddenly blown east (or maybe it was the Xanax kicking in that we took before boarding the plane from Puerto Rico). Whatever the reason, that mellow, laid-back feeling permeates everyone soon after arriving and gives Vieques its special character.

One of the Spanish Virgin Islands, Vieques lies seven miles east of Puerto Rico and is considered a municipality within the Commonwealth of Puerto Rico. *Viequenses*, as the almost 9,000 residents are called, are also U.S. citizens. About one-third of the island is owned by the U.S. Navy, which incredibly still uses it for live bombing practice (this means real bombs). Military maneuvers are executed from the huge Roosevelt Roads Naval Station, on the other side of the Pasaje de Vieques in Puerto Rico. Even napalm has been dropped on the island. The military presence, particularly the continued live bombing, has many locals furious (we would be, too!) and threatens to upset the wonderful ambience of the island. Most *viequenses* want the military totally out and all of the land turned into a park, reserve, or recreation area.

Tensions heightened in April 1999, when a civilian was killed and four were injured by two stray 500-pound bombs. This incident made the U.S. military presence a hot-button issue, not only in Vieques but in all of Puerto Rico. After the bombing accident, President Clinton commissioned a study to determine the need for a continued U.S. military presence in Vieques and Puerto Rico. The Navy gave up control of its former base on the west end of the island in May of 2001 under an agreement reached during the Clinton administration. Encompassing approximately 15,000 acres, the base was primarily used for support, ammunition storage, and housing for Navy personnel. Under the agreement, approximately 4,200 acres will be made available for local housing and other development. The remaining acreage, except for 100 acres still used by the Navy for its radar installation, is preserved as conservation land administered by the U.S. Fish and Wildlife Service and the Puerto Rican Conservation Trust. The conservation lands are open to the public, including the popular Green Beach. When you pass through the gate a security guard will ask for your license number and the plate number on your vehicle. Some areas within the conservation lands, however, are clearly marked as off-limits due to the presence of hazardous materials. Squeezed between the conservation lands on the west end and the U.S. Marines' Camp Garcia Maneuver Area on the east lies the civilian slice of the island. There are two towns on Vieques: Isabel II on the north side, the island's port and commercial center, and Esperanza, a smaller, mellower town on the south side geared more toward tourism. Of a total of about 55 square miles, only 17 are available for residential and commercial use. Even so, this part of Vieques seems uncrowded, unspoiled (no mega-resorts, fast-food chains, or traffic lights), and often very pretty. The island is hilly but lacks the big peaks to capture rain clouds (the highest summit is Mt. Pirata at 981 feet). Hence it is an arid island (about forty inches of rain fall annually) and a marked contrast to the El Yunque rain forest just 16 miles away in Puerto Rico. Vegetation here is similar to other Caribbean islands like Antigua and many of the Grenadines. Fortunately, water is piped in from the El Yunque watershed, so shower water pressure is good.

After a few days on the island, we noticed that an inordinate number of New Englanders, especially from Massachusetts and the Boston area, have moved here. Perhaps the no-frills air of Vieques appeals to our Yankee mentality, or maybe it was just that real estate was cheap. (Prices have risen considerably but are still cheaper than on many other islands.) We also noticed that outside of some outdoor activities like going to the beach, reading, exploring the island, and maybe diving or snorkeling, there's not a helluva lot to do here. This is fine if this is your intention. Another thing we noticed (we're *so* observant) is that none of the hotels are on a swimmable beach. It is necessary to rent a car and drive. We feel this may be an inconvenience for some. Visitors should also consider that the navy conducts training exercises or maneuvers up to 280 days a year. This fact can cause some kind of audio disturbance. President George W. Bush has promised the training exercises will end in 2003. Be sure to check with your hotel when making reservations to see if any major maneuvers are planned. Also be advised that due to the violent protests over the bombing issue and the tragedy of 9/11, the bases have been closed to all nonmilitary personnel. We are not sure when they will reopen. Finally, we noticed a lot of couples, which makes sense given the paucity of nightlife. It's definitely B.Y.O.B. (Bring Your Own Bedmate).

The Briefest History

The Taíno (Arawak) Indians first settled the island about 2500 B.C. and prospered until the arrival of Columbus in 1493. He named the island Vieques after its Taíno name *Bieques* ("Small Island") and claimed it for Spain. A series of rebellions and disease epidemics ensued, and by 1514 the Taínos were gone from the island, either enslaved on Puerto Rico or dead. Between 1514 and 1843, the island remained uninhabited and under the control of Spain's command post in Puerto Rico. As happened with most Caribbean islands, the

European powers all tried to get their hands on it. Colonization attempts were made by the English, Danish, and French, and all were repelled by the Spanish forces in Puerto Rico. During this period of skirmishes over Vieques, many pirates, sustained by seafood, shellfish, and fowl, called the island home.

Annoyed with other nations trying to capture the flag of Vieques, Spain finally made the island a Spanish municipality in 1843, and a fort was built and a colony begun. Prosperity followed in the form of sugar plantations worked by African slaves brought over from neighboring English islands (slavery was abolished in the English colonies in 1834 but not in Puerto Rico until 1873). In 1898 the Spanish-American War ceded the island to the U.S., which folded Vieques into the Commonwealth of Puerto Rico. At that time there were four *centrales* (sugar mills) in operation, owned by just a few families who didn't share their wealth. Worker conditions were deplorable and remained so until a general strike in 1915 improved the workers' situation significantly. Sugar and fishing sustained the island's economy until World War II.

With American involvement in the war inevitable, the U.S. Navy initiated a search for a training and maneuvers area that would be similar to the climate and conditions of the Japanese-occupied South Pacific. They found it on the east coast of Puerto Rico (Roosevelt Roads) and on Vieques. In 1941 70 percent of Vieques was expropriated, much to the chagrin of its 10,000-plus residents. The Navy land grab shut down the *centrales* (the last one closed in 1942). Construction jobs for the bases provided employment for a few years, but by 1945, 3,000 *viequenses* had been relocated to St. Croix. The rest were left in the middle section of the island with little or no employment opportunities. Thus the seeds of the anti-navy movement were sown. The live bombing and use of other lethal weapons on the island from World War II to the present accelerated the momentum. With the April 1999 incident, when the civilian was killed by a stray bomb, that movement is now at a fever pitch not only in Vieques but also in Puerto Rico.

While many *viequenses* sought economic opportunity in Puerto Rico or the States, the Puerto Rican government tried and failed several times to reestablish agriculture. Finally realizing that wasn't the way to go, they shifted the emphasis toward industry in the '60s.

With the added boost of Federal Tax Code 936, which gave U.S. companies huge tax breaks if they invested in and established plants or companies in Puerto Rico, the economic picture brightened in Vieques. The 1969 opening of the General Electric plant anchored the effort; it is still in operation today. Tourism on the island is a relatively recent phenomenon. In its infancy in the '80s, tourism accelerated into the '90s, as Vieques was "discovered" by both independent travelers and the media.

Vieques: Key Facts

LOCATION	18° N by 65° W
	7 miles east of Puerto Rico
	1,660 miles southeast of New York
SIZE	55 square miles
	21 miles long by 5 miles wide
HIGHEST POINT	Mt. Pirata (981 ft.)
POPULATION	9,000
LANGUAGE	Spanish (but most *viequenses* speak English)
TIME	Atlantic Standard time (1 hour ahead of EST, same as EDT)
AREA CODE	787 (Must be dialed before all local numbers as well.)
ELECTRICITY	110 volts AC, 60 cycles, same as U.S. and Canada
CURRENCY	The U.S. dollar
DRIVING	On the *right*
DOCUMENTS	None for Americans and no Customs hassles either; Canadians need proof of nationality or a passport; Brits need a passport and visa
DEPARTURE TAX	None
BEER TO DRINK	Medalla
RUM TO DRINK	Don Q or Bacardi
MUSIC TO HEAR	Salsa!
TOURISM INFO	787-741-5000
	www.vieques-island.com
	www.enchanted-isle.com/enchanted/Vieques.htm

Getting There

The most convenient way to get to Vieques is to fly from San Juan's Luis Muñoz Marín International Airport. **Vieques Air Link** (787-722-3736 in Isla Verde/San Juan or 888-901-9247) has three round-trip flights daily to Vieques's fairly new, modern terminal. Round-trip airfare is $135 for adults and $135 for children. Planes are of the small propeller variety, so early reservations are advised. The trip takes about thirty minutes. **Isla Nena Air Service** (888-263-6213 or 787-741-6362) also flies to Vieques from Marín International Airport. In addition, **Vieques Air Link** has scheduled service from San Juan's smaller, domestic Isla Grande Airport (just to the west of the Miramar section of San Juan and very convenient for anyone staying in the Condado or Old San Juan). Both airlines offer charter service.

Another option is to fly from Fajardo, which is an hour to an hour and a half east of San Juan (depending on traffic). This small airport has a lot more daily flights and they take only 10 minutes. Both **Vieques Air Link** and **Isla Nena Air Service** offer scheduled and charter service here. Finding the airport is a tad tricky, so pay attention to the airport signs and don't be afraid to ask for directions (it happens often here).

The Fajardo Port Authority also provides passenger and car ferry service three times daily to Vieques (787-863-4560 or 0705 in Fajardo and 787-741-4761 in Vieques). Passengers do not need reservations; the fare is $4 round-trip. Reservations are necessary for cars; fares are $26 round-trip for the car plus $4 for each passenger. The trip takes an hour.

Getting Around

Since you have to drive to get to a swimming beach in Vieques (especially the good ones), renting a car is a must. While the island roads are in good shape and are well marked, the naval base roads can get bumpy. We suggest renting a jeep for this reason—and because they're fun. Be sure to request one where you can take the soft top off (even more fun). Rentals range between $35 and $50 a day for jeeps and cars. Minivans are about $60. All rental companies are local, and most will arrange for airport pickup and drop-off (or will let you leave the car at the airport). Try **Island Car Rentals** (787-741-1666, e-mail: islandcar@aol.com), **Steve's Car Rentals** (787-741-8135), **Maritza's Car Rentals** (787-741-0078), or **Dreda & Fonsin's Rent-A-Car** (787-741-8163).

Focus on Vieques: Mellowing Out on the Beaches

We know that's a very '70s expression—"mellow out"—and we really have tried to erase that decade from our collective memory, but the term is really what Vieques is all about. How does one do that? Well, just staying here will automatically start you on the path. Reading, sleeping, and maybe a few cocktails will help. Lying or walking on the beach and swimming in the clear turquoise water wouldn't hurt either.

There are a lot of undeveloped beaches to explore. While Vieques lacks the truly stunning beaches of its sister Culebra, or of St. John or Anguilla, most visitors will be very pleased with the more than 50 options available (we're more than a little jaded, so it takes a lot to impress us). Our favorite beaches are Sun Bay, Media Luna, and Navio Beach. All hotels provide directions to the island's beaches, which, with one exception (Green Beach), are on the south side of the island.

Sun Bay is just east of the center of Esperanza and wins the prize for best beach on Vieques. A long, palm-fringed crescent of white sand with good swimming areas (many of the island's beaches have shallow coral reefs close to the water's edge), Sun Bay also has picnic tables, bathroom facilities, and a sandy road that runs parallels to it. The best part is on the left (eastern) end of the beach, where it's calmer and there is good snorkeling. You can also camp at Sun Bay; call 787-741-8198 for more information. Media Luna and Navio Beach are accessed from the bumpy, sandy road at Sun Bay. **Media Luna** is fairly secluded and has shade trees, shallow calm water, and good snorkeling (again on the eastern side). **Navio Beach** is small, very secluded, is framed by rocky bluffs; has the most turqoise water and often has body-surfable waves. Some bathers take it all off here. Be advised that there is no shade, so bring an umbrella.

On the east end of the island is Camp García. Here, on the south coast, are Red, Blue, and García beaches, but since the protest over the training maneuvers and the tragic events of 9/11, the base is now closed to the public. We are not sure if and when they will re-open.

On the east end, is **Green Beach**. This faces Puerto Rico and has great views of El Yunque. However, stick to weekdays here; on weekends boaters from Fajardo anchor at Green Beach and it gets crowded. Sheltered from the trade winds, the beach can get buggy by mid-afternoon if it has rained recently.

Where to Stay

Since the 136-room and 20-suite deluxe Martineau Bay Resort won't be opening due to the withdrawal of its investors, Vieques hasn't lost any of its innocence. The island is still a place of small inns, guest houses, and villa rentals.

Hacienda Tamarindo, P.O. Box 1569, Route 996, Km 4.5, Vieques, PR 00765. Local: 787-741-8525, fax 787-741-3215.
Web site: www.enchanted-isle.com/tamarindo
e-mail: hactam@aol.com

We adore the Hacienda Tamarindo, a 16-room Spanish-style inn, opened in 1997, set on breezy rising grounds with sweeping views of sloping pastures and the Caribbean. Ex-Vermonters Linda and Burr Vail built *and* opened the inn in an amazingly short time considering the difficulties of building and running a business in the Caribbean *and* on a small island. With it they've created an extraordinarily comfortable and warm environment. They are a very amiable and hospitable couple, and their friendly and helpful style as innkeepers is one of the great things about the Hacienda. So is the 40-something-foot tamarind tree growing smack dab in the middle of the inn (it graces the Hacienda's atrium and dining terrace). The Vail's collection of art, collectibles, and antiques acquired during years in Vermont adorn both the public spaces and the guest rooms. An honor bar in the lobby provides refreshment, and there is an air-conditioned lounge with TV-VCR and library. Outside, a pretty pool with chaises provides a place to take a dip and get some sun. Be sure to say hello to the talking parrot. He'll give you an earful!

Each of the rooms has its own style and décor (Linda was a commercial interior designer), and all feature mahogany louvered doors and windows, terra-cotta-tiled floors, ceiling fans, and baths with tiled showers. A suite comes with a Jacuzzi tub and private lanai. The Hacienda is also wheelchair accessible. A full American breakfast is served on the second-floor dining terrace (we loved the real Vermont maple syrup on the table). The Inn on the Blue Horizon's Café Blu is just down the hill for dinner.

Rates are *Pricey* and up (full American breakfast). No children under 15 are allowed (that means no screaming kids and stroller obstacles—we like that!).

Inn on the Blue Horizon, P.O. Box 1556, Route 996, Km 4.5, Vieques, PR 00765. Local: 787-741-3318, fax 787-741-0522. Web site: www.innonthebluehorizon.com e-mail: blue_inn@compuserve.com

The first time we visited the Inn on the Blue Horizon in 1996, there were only three rooms and Café Blu, the island's best restaurant. Now there are nine rooms at this wonderful place, and the restaurant has been renamed Chef Michael's. The owners have plans to build 14 three-bedroom villas. The inn, set on 20 acres and owned by ex–New Yorkers James Weis and Billy Knight, is beautifully decorated—to within an inch of its life. Common areas have big overstuffed sofas and chairs; antiques, art, and open space abound. Books and magazines are placed just so, and dramatic flower arrangements are strategically located throughout the inn. It's like a page out of *Architectural Digest*. There is a library, crammed with books. A pretty pool surrounded by a terra-cotta-tiled deck faces the sea and is bordered by a hibiscus hedge. There's even a tiny gym for the gym bunnies among us. With all this studied stylishness comes a slight attitude, but since we can give it, too (only when deserved, of course), it didn't bother us a bit.

Not surprisingly, the guest rooms (three in the main house and the other six sharing three cottages) are extremely tasteful. Most have four-poster beds; all rooms have queen- or king-size beds, except one, which has an antique double four-poster. All rooms except for the suite in the main house are air conditioned and are also cooled by the steady trade winds and ceiling fans. All have antiques, terra-cotta-tiled floors, a color scheme of warm muted tones, bright upholstery and fabrics, all-cotton linens, cut flowers, glass-block showers, and spacious lanais with white wooden chairs (in the cottage units). Our favorite rooms were called Mariana and Esperanza. We felt the Joseph and Judith rooms in the back cottage, while very pretty, did not have as good a view of the sea as the other cottage rooms. The original three main-house rooms have high ceilings, four-poster beds, and very dramatic drapes. Thoughtful touches in the rooms include a beach umbrella and chairs, cooler and thermos, beach towels, flashlight, and bug spray.

Rates are **Very** *Pricey* and up (CP). No children under 14 allowed.

The Crow's Nest, P.O. Box 1521, Route 201, Km 1.6, Vieques, PR 00765. Local: 787-741-0033, fax 787-741-1294.
Web site: www.crowsnestvieques.com
e-mail: thenest@coqui.net

The epitome of what Vieques used to be (very casual, no frills, laid-back, and inexpensive), the Crow's Nest has 16 units. Seven are rented as condos, and nine as hotel rooms. which are actually condos rented out by the inn. With new owners Scott Bowie and Eli Belendez, this five-acre inland property sits on a hillside with sweeping views to the north of Vieques Sound and Culebra. The Crow's Nest boasts one of Vieques's best restaurants, island Café, and a friendly bar, too. There is a pool and a lounge area.

The units, all freshly painted, are studios with kitchenettes, ceiling fans, air conditioning, coolers, and beach towels and chairs. Scott and Eli also plan to add phones with data ports to all rooms. Some units have a balcony or private terrace. Best of all, it won't break the bank to stay here.

Rates are *Cheap* (CP). No children under 12 allowed.

La Finca Caribe, P.O. Box 1332, Route 995, Km 2.5, Vieques, PR 00765. U.S.: 206-567-5656. Local: 787-741-0495, fax 787-741-3584.
Web site: www.lafinca.com
e-mail: lafinca@merwincreative.com

Formerly the very funky women's retreat known as New Dawn, La Finca Caribe is definitely a different kind of lodging experience. While no longer just a women's retreat, La Finca is still funky. Think Indian print bedspreads, summer camp, Birkenstocks, pajama parties, rustic communal living, hammocks, and the music of James Taylor all rolled into one and you have an image of what this place is like. With the addition of some paint and a much needed swimming pool (curiously saltwater despite the fact that La Finca is way up in the hills and three miles from the beach), it's certainly in better shape than the New Dawn ever was. But if you have an aversion to plywood, you won't like it here—the exterior and the floors are just that. However, there is a good-size porch with hammocks, and all showers are outdoors (and enclosed, of course).

The six rooms in the main house share two baths. All have mosquito nets, white walls and whitewashed floors, wall hangings, Indian print upholstery, and not a lot of privacy. There are two separate cabañas: one with a separate bedroom and private bath and the other a studio with sleeping loft. There are no TVs or phones in the rooms and cabañas. There is a communal kitchen in the main house. The entire place can be rented to a group and sleeps twenty.

Rates are **Cheap** and up (EP).

La Casa de Francés, P.O. Box 458, Vieques, PR 00765. Local: 787-741-3751, fax 787-741-2330.
Web site: www.enchanted-isle.com/LaCasa
e-mail: greenbla@coqui.net

Once *the* place to stay on Vieques, all we can say is "What happened?" The best thing about La Casa is the name of the bar—the "Prozac Patio" (it speaks our language). Occupying a striking hundred-year-old plantation mansion, benign neglect has prevented it from realizing its potential. Owner and curmudgeon (by his own admission) Irving Greenblatt seems content to let it be. Rumor has it, the inn has been sold to an Italian owner who plans to totally refurbish it. There are 19 rooms, six in an annex with air conditioning and very plain. The 12 rooms in the main house have high ceilings, mismatched upholstery, and linoleum floors! There are verandas off the rooms and small tiled baths. There is a swimming pool and some kind of altar on the grounds as you enter. *We* wouldn't stay here, but if you like eccentricity, search no more.

Rates are *Not So Cheap* (CP).

Trade Winds Guest House and Restaurant, P.O. Box 1012, 107 Calle Flamboyan, Malecón, Esperanza, Vieques, PR 00765. Local: 787-741-8666, fax 787-741-2964.
Web site: www.enchanted-isle.com/tradewinds
e-mail: tradewns@coqui.net

Located right in Esperanza on the western end of the Malecón, this is a fairly modern, motelish lodging with an affordable price tag and a convenient location. Its shortage of ambiance and direct location on the malecón make it a less desirable place to stay. There are 11 rooms, all with private bath and ceiling fans. Some rooms also have air conditioning, kitchenettes, and lanais.

Rates are *Cheap* (EP).

Casa Cielo, P.O. Box 310, Route 995 Km 1.1, Vieques, PR 00765. Local: 787-741-2403, fax 787-741-2403.
Website: www.enchanted-isle.com/casacielo
Email: cielo@coqui.net

We weren't kidding about former New Englanders living on Vieques. This nine-room inn with commanding views of the Vieques coastline to the south has two new owners from the Bay State: JoAnne Hamilton and Jim Ducharme. *Architectural Digest* from the 1960s is the simplest way to describe the inn's contemporary design. Actually, once a private home, it was converted into an inn by an architect who knocked down the outside walls facing the water and built extended, wraparound decks on the ground and second levels. They provide room for a large pool and plenty of open-air seating for taking in the sweeping views. And do we mean sweeping. This inn may just have the best views on the island. The architecture includes lots of glass, so there's plenty to see from the inside, too. The design includes a common room with atrium on the second level with a full kitchen available to the guests. Standard rooms come with balcony and are simply furnished with white walls. Some are air conditioned. All have ceiling fans. One room is handicap accessible. We only wish the driveway were more accessible, as well, and we recommend a 4WD vehicle or intrepid driver for the trip up.

Rates are *Pricey* and up.

Villa Rentals

For groups or families, a villa rental is probably your best bet, and there is a good selection from which to choose. Two reputable companies can find the right place for you and can help with other island details as well. Contact:

Connections / Jane Sabin Real Estate, P.O. Box 358, 117 Calle Munoz Rivera, Vieques, PR 00765. Local: 787-741-0023, fax 787-741-2022.
Web site: www.enchanted-isle.com/Connections
e-mail: ctorrey@coqui.net

Crow's Nest Realty. P.O. Box 1409, Vieques, PR 00765. Local: 787-741-2843, fax 787-741-1294.
e-mail: sheilaslevin@compuserve.com
e-mail: crowsnestrealty@msn.com

Where to Eat

For such a small place, there are a surprising number of restaurants. Here are our picks:

Bananas, Calle Flamboyán, Malecón, Esperanza, 741-8700. This fun, casual open-air restaurant (of course there's a roof) is a local gathering spot and a great place to hang and work on some margaritas. It looks out on the Malecón and the sea beyond. The menu is pub fare: steaks, grilled seafood, and their famous burgers. Open daily for lunch and dinner until 10 or 11 P.M. (depending on business). $$

Café Media Luna, 351 A. G. Mellado, Isabel II, 741-2594. Located in downtown Isabel II, this restaurant in a restored house offers a creative international menu by chef Monica Chitnis. The cafe has live music once a month on a Saturday night. Open Wednesday to Sunday, 7 to 10:30 P.M. Only open off-season on Friday through Sunday. $$$

Chef Michael's, Inn on the Blue Horizon, Route 996, Km 4.5, Esperanza, 741-3318 & 741-0527. At the island's best restaurant, chef Michael Glatz creates an inventive fusion menu from different cuisines of the world. Its octagonal bar is a pleasant place for a drink. Open Thursday to Monday, 6 to 10 P.M. Reservations advised. $$$$$

Chez Shack, Route 995, Km 8.6, 741-2175. A funky collection of brightly painted tin shacks orginally built around 1910. Just down the road from La Finca Caribe, Chez Shack serves a great menu of local dishes and seafood and has a very popular barbecue on Monday nights—mesquite grill featuring lobster, shrimp, steak, lamb, and fish and a salad bar. Open daily 6 until 11 P.M. or so. $$$

Island Cafe at the Crow's Nest, Route 201, Km 1.6, 741-0011. The popular restaurant at the Crow's Nest has made a few changes. Hurricane Georges took off the restaurant's back roof, which has been replaced, and a new open deck has been added to the front. New owners chefs Owen Trilley and Jason Humphries also operate the Oasis Restaurant at the Water's Edge Guesthouse in Isabel II. Their menu features ribs, burgers, and sandwiches. Open 6 to 10 P.M. daily. Closed Tuesday and every other Wednesday. $$

La Campasina, Barrio La Hueca, Route 201, Esperanza, 741-1239. This small restaurant nestled beneath a roofed patio at the side of the road is an island tradition of more than 20 years. The tree-house-like setting is intimate and unpretentious. The menu features pork, steak, and seafood. The bar is set around an enormous boulder. Open daily 6 to 10 P.M. $$

Don't Miss

Bioluminescence Bay—Located at both Mosquito and Barracuda, these are two of the few bioluminescent bays in the world. There was also one in La Parguera, Puerto Rico, but fail-

ure to protect its fragile ecosystem led to a fading of its biolumi-
nescence. In the dark of a calm night, phosphorescent plankton
(dinoflagellates, to be precise) create "sparks" with any vigorous
movement in the water, which disturbs their nesting. Captain
Sharon Grasso of **Island Adventures, Inc.** (787-741-0720,
www.boibay.com) has been giving tours to the bay for the last 10
years. The one-and-a half-hour tour on her new pontoon boat
includes swimming and stargazing. Departure time is around
6:30 P.M. and rates are about $20 per person.

Snorkeling and Diving—Vieques has some great dive sites and a
full-service dive operation. Call the **Blue Caribe Dive Center**
(741-2522) in Esperanza. Captain Richard Barone of **Vieques
Nature Tours** has a glass bottom boat and offers snorkeling and
education tours (787-741-1980).

Fuerte Conde de Mirasol—The fort in Isabel II was the last to be
built by a colonial power in the Western Hemisphere (it was
built in the 1840s). It has been restored and houses interesting
island exhibits, art, and the Vieques Historic Archives. Open
Wednesday to Sunday from 10 A.M. to 4 P.M. or by special
appointment. Call 787-741-1717.

INDEX

Write to Rum & Reggae

Dear *Rum & Reggae Caribbean* Readers,

We really do appreciate and value your comments, suggestions, or information about anything new or exciting in the Caribbean. We'd love to hear about your experiences, good and bad, while you were in the tropics. Your feedback helps us shape the next edition. So please let us hear from you. Here's how:

>Visit our Web site at: www.rumreggae.com
>e-mail us at yahmon@rumreggae.com
>or write to:

>Mr. Yah Mon
>Rum & Reggae Guidebooks
>P.O. Box 152
>Prides Crossing, MA 01965

>Sincerely,
>*Jonathan Runge*

P.S.—We often mention cocktails, drinking, and other things in this book. We certainly do not mean to offend any nondrinkers or those in recovery. Please don't take offense—rum and its relatives are not a requirement for a successful vacation in the Caribbean.

The Author

JONATHAN RUNGE is the author of ten other travel books: *Rum & Reggae's Caribbean* (2002), *Rum & Reggae's Puerto Rico* (2002), *Rum & Reggae's Dominican Republic* (2002), *Rum & Reggae's Cuba* (2002), *Rum & Reggae's Hawai'i* (2001), *Rum & Reggae's Caribbean* 2000, *Rum & Reggae's Caribbean: The Insider's Guide to the Caribbean* (1993); *Hot on Hawai'i, The Definitive Guide to the Aloha State* (1989); *Rum & Reggae, What's Hot and What's Not in the Caribbean* (1988); and *Ski Party! The Skier's Guide to the Good Life,* co-authored with Steve Deschenes (1985). Jonathan has written for *Men's Journal, Outside, National Geographic Traveler, Out, Skiing, Boston,* and other magazines. Future books to be published in 2002 from Jonathan Runge include *Rum & Reggae's Brasil.*